At Mama's Knee

At Mama's Knee

Mothers and Race in
Black and White

April Ryan

ROWMAN & LITTLEFIELD
Lanham • Boulder • New York • London

Published by Rowman & Littlefield
A wholly owned subsidiary of The Rowman & Littlefield Publishing Group, Inc.
4501 Forbes Boulevard, Suite 200, Lanham, Maryland 20706
www.rowman.com

Unit A, Whitacre Mews, 26-34 Stannary Street, London SE11 4AB

Distributed by NATIONAL BOOK NETWORK

British Library Cataloguing in Publication Information Available

Library of Congress Cataloging-in-Publication Data
978-1-4422-6563-9 (cloth)
978-1-4422-6564-6 (electronic)

∞™ The paper used in this publication meets the minimum requirements of American National Standard for Information Sciences—Permanence of Paper for Printed Library Materials, ANSI/NISO Z39.48-1992.

Printed in the United States of America

Contents

Foreword   vii

Introduction   1

1   More Than a Headline   5

2   Born a Statistic   17

3   A Mother's Love   35

4   The N-Word   47

5   The Faith of Our Mothers   65

6   Mothers, Presidents, and Race   81

7   A Tale of Two Cities   87

8   Assimilation   99

9   Work-Life Balance   109

10   Educating the Future   117

Conclusion—A Prayer for Harmony   123

Acknowledgments   127

Index   129

About the Author   137

Foreword

$\mathcal{I}$ hope you've seen April Ryan on *Hardball*. She's one of the stars of the program. Informed, passionate and totally in the moment, she brings joy as well as sharp reporting. Most of you know that already. The fact is we have a lot of fun, not just on air but during commercials when you're not watching. Our lively conversation gets going before we even get out of the make-up room.

But there is a serious side to my colleague, deadly serious. When the topic goes to what's happening on the streets of this country, she's not kidding around. When it comes to the dangers facing young African Americans, it's life and death.

Telling their story in these pages is April Ryan, my colleague in national journalism. Here she writes from experience about life in a city she heads back to after covering the politics of Washington.

In the spring of 2015, Baltimore had its own big story to tell. It was the pictures of Freddie Gray being hauled into a Baltimore police wagon. It was the relentless TV footage of rioting teens racing across streets, smashing store windows, challenging police lines.

How do you save your children from all of that? That's the question April Ryan asks. You're coming home from work in the nation's capital, driving through these same troubled Baltimore streets. How do you protect your own from this?

In *At Mama's Knee: Mothers and Race in Black and White*, Ryan lays it out for us. She lets grown-up children tell how they were raised on streets just like these. We hear from President Barack Obama, Senator Cory Booker, Valerie Jarrett, also from mothers who couldn't save their children no matter how hard they tried. We learn of the "unique grace" of the author's own mother.

We learn, too, about "The Talk." It's when an African American father takes his young son aside and tells him the facts of life for African Americans, how a single encounter with police can be deadly.

For many of us, this is something we've never had to deal with. Our dad told my brothers and I to say "officer" if we got stopped driving. Being polite and respectful was a way to avoid a ticket. April Ryan and other parents have to give such warnings if only to keep their kids from getting killed.

There's something basic here. Young people think everything they do is brand new, that they're the first person who ever did it. Parents know differently. They've seen it all before, maybe tried it themselves. They desperately try to warn of the trouble to come. It's hard and sometimes it just doesn't work.

But it's the parents' God-given place to try.

Ryan writes, "As my mother would tell me, a good mother is her child's biggest supporter and the harshest critic, able to speak truth when needed, and support even when unwanted."

"For Black people, society has taught us we must prepare our children because if we don't, the world will teach the lessons with no compassion."

This is a book for all to read. It's about tough love where the stakes are life and death.

Read what my colleague has to say. The stranger this world is to us, the more important it is for us to learn it.

Chris Matthews
Host of MSNBC's *Hardball*

Introduction

*F*or the past fifteen-plus years, from pregnancy to giving birth, I have never felt more responsibility in any capacity than that of being a mother. Looking back over the journey of motherhood, it is incredible! There are days I want to shout from the mountaintops about the marvels of being the mother of two wonderfully talented girls. On some other days the challenges are hard, and I even wonder if I have the stamina for the long haul. But I am built for this. I am a mother! What a great and God-given reward.

The job of a mother is tremendous. I found that out when I delivered my first child. After a very difficult pregnancy and then years later, while attempting to make ends meet, I seriously pondered how my mother was able to pull it all together and do it with a smile.

I am so grateful I was afforded the chance to tell my mother "thank you" for her mothering and her great example. We had that conversation years before her death. I never understood how she did it, calmly and with her unique grace. It wasn't easy, as I was a very excitable child and am still excitable today! After she figured out how to handle me, she doubled her love of children seven years later with the birth of my baby brother. That baby brother is now towering more than one full foot in height over his big sister. How funny is that?

But getting back to my thankful conversation with my mom, I told her "thank you" for all of the advice, from teaching me about the how-tos of tax season all the way to forming our private two-member stock investment club to how to build my business. My mother, from the moment I was born, was with me every step of the way. In fact, we were so close that we talked several times a day. We talked about everything. My mother wanted to make sure I was ready for the world. Just in daily conversation, my mother would discuss current events and, in some instances, how race played a big part in many issues. My mother wanted me to live in a world of equality, yet understand the realities of the present day. The reality is that we are Black. She offered historical notes about what our Blackness has encountered, but she also offered pride in our contributions, the contributions that so many Black people have given to the world. When we were in the car, she would remind us that Garrett Morgan, an African American inventor, is credited with creating the traffic light . . . and the gas mask. She also told us about Charles Drew who helped shape our current blood donation system, and George Washington Carver and his agricultural advance with the peanut. She and my father worked hard to give me and my brother a life that was more diverse and afforded more opportunities than what they were afforded. However, she also wanted her children to be mindful and aware of who we are. My mother spoke of race with the facts, and it always came straight from the heart.

Race can be legislated, but it is really a heart issue. As the Bible says, "As a man thinketh so is he." So who better to help us navigate the waters of this sometimes-murky issue than mothers, as they are a child's first teacher, nurturer, protector, and influencer? A mother's love is awe-inspiring, but the power does not always have to come from a birth mother. You will read in these pages of women who have given birth and some who have not, but who still have helped in "the village and the sisterhood" of mothers and how they can and do shape the mind-set of generations.

In April 2015, I saw a reflection of myself in one Baltimore mother whose instincts during the riots went viral. During the infamous Baltimore riots, I found myself hysterical with the actions of the kids and young adults in my hometown of Baltimore. I was asking, "Where are the parents?" the entire time while watching and listening to what was happening. One mother rose up and defied the law and stood, with cameras rolling, and enacted corporal punishment on her only son. I applaud her and her actions. She was trying to save her son from the madness and mayhem of that day. As my mother would tell me, a good mother is her child's biggest supporter and harshest critic, able to speak truth when needed and support even when unwanted. In this book, many people share their stories and their experiences as Black people, particularly Black mothers, raising a family despite the challenges. This book opened my heart to understanding that everyone's story is not the same, but yet just as powerful as the next. And that is what links us all together.

We look at who we are as people. Much of that comes, for better or worse, from the influence of mothers. The best part of me comes from the gentle kindness of my mother, and that best part of me flows into my two daughters. It is generational, more than just a handing down of recipes, jewelry, or clothes. We hand down our values, dreams, and aspirations to those next generations. I can't help but think of my mother's mother, and her mother before her, and her mother before her. For me, those generations flourished with the hope of new generations, as I do for my daughters, Ryan and Grace. There's a generational link from them to me and then from me to my mother, Mary Vivian Gowans Ryan, to her mother, Etta Viola Smith Gowans, to her mother, Ida Brown Smith, to her mother, Laura Brown, who was married to the last known slave in my family, Joseph Dollar Brown. And your family may be very similar, or entirely different, but what I hope you take from the stories in this book is that we can certainly learn from and appreciate each other despite our challenges, especially as Black people in this country.

I can't talk about mothers without offering my story. A story that I very rarely speak of, because in my job as a White House correspondent, it's my job to interview and share the stories of others, never my own. It has taken almost ten years for me to be able to openly reveal my heart as it relates to my mother. She planned to retire and work with me in growing my company and to ultimately manage my career. She was going to retire after her forty-two years at Morgan State University and put our plan into motion. Unfortunately, life threw us a curve. She died in 2007, leaving me and the rest of my family and our broader community to pick up the pieces. But what I remember and pass on to my children is how dedicated she was. I also remember my last words to my mother and hers to me. I told her I loved her and she, knowing death was imminent, immediately said, "I love you back!" However, those words are sacred to me, as I only offer them to my children when they tell me they love me. I tell them, like my mother told me, "I love you back."

From the time we found out she was going to die, she was given three months to live, but she was able to last for six. My father was in shock and disbelief, but it may have been due to his possible neurological issues. However, those six months were the most beautiful time of my life. I stood with my mother as her advocate with the doctors and helped her coordinate her large number of siblings for the bone marrow transplant that never happened. I helped her with the process of paying her bills while she sat in her hospital bed. At times we even found laughter as we hoped she would survive this horrible disease called leukemia. We picked out a wig for her to use after the chemotherapy resulted in massive hair loss. I was pregnant with my last child at that time. My mother said, "I am not afraid to die, but I want to see my grandchildren grow." My mother was a grandmother twice before her death, with my daughter Ryan and my brother's daughter, who was born right when my mother fell ill. Her illness prevented her from seeing the latest reflection of her, her baby granddaughter Ella.

But what was so wonderful was that women of all races, particularly mothers, came in and supported me after my mother's passing. It wasn't just family. The instinct to care kicked in. Although I was grown and a mother myself, the mothering instincts of other women came naturally, because they understood the magnitude of the loss. I lost my Queen. My mother.

My mother brought me into this world and stood *with* me and stood *for* me every day until her last breath. There was no other option for me. I had to stand with her now. During that six-month window, she told me how proud of me she was and that I was everything she had hoped for. My mother would always tell me, throughout my life, that she had wished for me when she was twelve years old on her family's farm in Cerro Gordo, North Carolina. She even had my name already picked out at that young age. And when she was a married adult, she went home for her grandmother's funeral in 1966 and boldly told them that when they would see her again she would have April. And that came to pass. When she made the statement, she walked in faith, hoping for that baby girl she had longed for since the age of twelve.

I wish that everyone has had an experience with their mom like I did. Yes, I was hardheaded and determined in many instances to do things my way. But with a loving hand, she guided me through my successes and missteps, all the while loving me. Her example has been a strong one that I work to follow as a single parent. Everyone has a story of their mother or of someone who was a mother figure to them.

Parenthood is sacred. Women have been given a gift of something special. We offer the birth of generations and the emotional nurturing of those we guide. And it is usually left to the mother to teach her children about the ways of the world. That means that no subject can be left to chance. Everything must be discussed, because it can be a matter of life or death.

It's an important topic for all of us to deal with, regardless of who we are. If we are to make real strides together as a nation, everyone needs to play a part, no matter what race you are and regardless of your sexual orientation or religious beliefs. It's especially important for our Black youth, because as we have seen time and again, they are on the front lines of this racial inequality. So it's my hope that this book will help to broach the topic that we often shy away from for so many reasons. But we can't avoid it anymore.

We must teach our children, whether with words or actions, about race in America.

• 1 •

More Than a Headline

Traditionally in the American Black community, there is an instinctive coming-of-age truth for our young Black men called "the talk." It is something Black fathers or father figures give their sons or equivalents. It's meant to be a lifetime tool that might help these boys strategically navigate interactions with law enforcement, with the ultimate goal of avoiding altercations. That "talk" can spell life or death for some Black males. I know it sounds so 1950s and '60s, but now, more than ever, that's the reality in the modern age more than sixty years later. The essence of "the talk" is a dad telling his son in blunt terms that some bad policing results in death for our Black men and boys. Be it intentional or unintentional, it is more than a soulful truth—it's an unavoidable fact in our communities.

When I was on a tour promoting my first book, *The Presidency in Black and White*, I was amazed at how White people responded to a May 30, 2015, *Washington Post* newspaper article detailing the number of murders of Black males by police. The story was titled "Fatal Police Shootings in 2015 Approaching 400 Nationwide." Those statistics represented just the first few months of 2015, not even six months. In Charlottesville, Virginia, a questioner asked me if I was shocked by the stats in that article. I said very nonchalantly, "No." The questioner was stunned by my attitude and approach to his question. Seeing his amazement, I explained, "I am the daughter of a Black man and the sister of a Black man." I also admitted that I had, myself, been racially profiled by police. We call it "Driving While Black." This experience is so common in Black life that it's referred to as "DWB." More than anything, I'm a part of the Black community that consistently beats the drum when these crimes happen. We express our pain and hurt through talking to one another, spreading the stories, and at the same time, we try to come to grips with the inconceivable pain that happens over and over in our communities.

The stories of Black males being killed by police have been detailed for decades in the Black media and by word of mouth. Only recently has the mainstream media begun to tell the tale, finally building to a collective crescendo when the nation is appalled and wants instant updates. The world is just waking up to this fact of police being involved in shootings, largely because of the proliferation of video cameras and cell phones. These have allowed bystanders to capture the gruesome and graphic deaths of young men like Michael Brown, Eric Garner, Freddie Gray, and Tamir Rice. The Internet has allowed for instant uploads so thousands of people can share and reshare videos on their social media pages, to the point where the media can't ignore these events. The scales of justice may have finally begun to tip due to a heightened awareness, but there is, of course, a long road ahead for all of us.

The increased public interest in these events has created a demand that can't be ignored. This has resulted in every angle of these stories being explored and reported on by Black media, but also by traditional outlets. This became particularly so after the public heard the actual sounds of an armed neighborhood watchman/vigilante killing a Black teenager named Trayvon Martin in Sanford, Florida, on February 26, 2012. The local media from Sanford initially discussed the shooting without using the name of the victim or the suspect, but they did include what happened behind the gates of that secluded community. However, this time something was different. For whatever reason, the story grew locally, and two weeks later, according to the *New York Times*, CBS picked up the story. Then it gained national momentum, ultimately receiving attention and a Rose Garden statement from President Barack Obama.

The glaring spotlight on the issues of racial profiling, "Driving While Black," and the deep divisions of mistrust between the Black community and law enforcement could not be denied by anyone in this country or by spectators around the world. The nation, not just Black America, was realizing the ugly truth of our pain.

In 2016, the day of the memorial service for the Dallas police officers shot by a retaliatory gunman, Jeh Johnson of Homeland Security explained during my radio interview with him that tensions between the community and the police happen to be a "national security issue." He said that when there is a perceived breach in trust, there is little chance of working together to make a change. Cooperation between the public and law enforcement is crucial for the success of campaigns such as "if you see something, say something."

Because of the proliferation of events like the killing of Trayvon Martin, the message of these traditional talks that Black fathers give their sons has to evolve. Also, with the new Black family dynamic of women being the heads of the households as single parents, we as mothers have to give this talk to our sons as well as our daughters.

The catch-22 of the situation is that those Black fathers might have remained in the family unit had it not been for the increased instances of police violence, which have resulted in a disproportionate number of Black men—fathers and sons—behind bars or worse, dead. According to an April 20, 2015, *New York Times* article, by Justin Wolfers, David Leonhardt, and Kevin Quealy, titled "1.5 Million Missing Black Men," for every 100 Black women not in jail, there are only 83 Black men. The remaining men—1.5 million of them—are, in a sense, missing. As the story explains, "They are missing, largely because of early deaths or because they are behind bars."

The Pew Research Center says four in ten American households with children under age eighteen now include a mother who is either the sole or the primary earner for her family. This share, the highest on record, has quadrupled since 1960. And the US Census Bureau's report of American families and living arrangements in 2012 shows the following demographic characteristics of these households: Black children (55 percent) and Hispanic children (31 percent) were more likely to live with one parent than non-Hispanic White children (21 percent) or Asian children (13 percent).

For most of us, our mother was our first teacher. She taught us the basics and was the first person we learned to trust as she offered guidance with her nurturing spirit. For many in the Black community, their mother taught them critical survival skills. She told her children not to dig in their pockets or fiddle in their purses while in a store, as the store owner might suspect them of shoplifting.

I discovered just how a mother influences her children's development on August 4, 2015. That day, in the Green Room of the White House, I interviewed FUBU founder and CEO Daymond John for President Obama's "Demo Day." It was a day spotlighting innovation and invention, with a particular push for minorities and women to get more involved as entrepreneurs. John, at the time, was President Obama's Global Ambassador for Entrepreneurship. Just a few days before, he had traveled to Kenya with the president to talk and mentor about entrepreneurship. John told me that his mother was the key to his success. He began the start-up business that is now FUBU literally in his mother's basement. He reflected, saying, "A mom is the ultimate start-up. A mom, she has a child. There is no blueprint there. She is going to figure it out. The buck stops with her."

This multimillionaire investor was right. There is no blueprint or textbook on how to properly perform this all-encompassing job of mothering Black children, but each of us figures it out in our own way, hoping for the best and working hard to step around or jump over the worst.

Take Sybrina Fulton for example, Trayvon Martin's mother. She was no different than any other mother wanting the best for her kids—a good education, a happy childhood, and a successful transition into adulthood. But life dealt her a cold blow. Fulton felt the ugly truth of racial profiling even as her sons were brought up in the Miami area in an integrated community. As a single mother, she gave her two Black sons, her pride and joy, "the talk." Her "talk" started with how her own mother dealt with matters of race. Fulton told her sons how her mother instilled compassion in her for all people, which made sense to her, since her mother was eminently fair and just on matters of race.

Fulton says she followed in her mother's footsteps: "I just have compassion for people regardless of the color of their skin." Like her mother, Fulton was born and raised in the Miami area. She wanted a bright future for her boys, Jahvaris and Trayvon. Both boys attended mixed-race middle and high schools after being taken out of predominantly Black schools. Fulton explained, "I made sure. I wanted them to have the best education they could and so I ended up transferring them from the school they were supposed to go to in the area and had them go to another school so they could get a better education."

That change in schools for Trayvon and his brother fostered Sybrina Fulton's "talk" on race with her sons. Like the increasing numbers of women (particularly Black women) who are now heading their households, her conversation on race with her children was a matter of survival. Fulton began her conversation while her kids were in middle school, and like many African American parents, planned to continue building on that "talk" throughout their childhoods. It was not a "hate" conversation, she remembers. She says, "It was not filled with a bad tone . . . just a conversation for them to realize who they were as young men, and to show others may view you differently as to who you are." Fulton reiterated, "It was not an ill tone or anything with a bad intent."

Ironically for Black people, society has taught us that we must prepare our children, because if we don't, the world will teach the lessons, with no compassion, as we have seen in some highly publicized cases. Valerie Jarrett, Senior Advisor to President Obama, said, "I've had colleagues who've said to me they had no idea about the conversation that Black parents have with their Black boys. . . . They had no idea."

Many decades ago, an Alabama mother, who loved her ten children all the same, chose a different route for informing her offspring about the harsh realities of being Black in the South. Indirectly, this mother's actions became the catalyst for one of her children to become a key figure in this nation's fight for civil rights. This mother was Willa Mae Lewis. She was also a wife and a sharecropper. She helped oversee her own family's land, 110 acres that her husband purchased for $300. The family still owns that land today.

Willa Mae Lewis never had actual talks about race with her children, but that didn't stop her young, inquisitive son, John Robert Lewis, from asking questions. Now the 5th District Georgia congressman, Lewis remembers asking his mother in 1954—around the time of *Brown vs. Board of Education*—about racist "Whites Only" signs that would pop up around their community. His mother would look him directly in the eye and tell him not to be "so nosy." Back then many in the South accepted the racial conditions of the time because it seemed like nothing was going to change, so why "rock the boat"?

Lewis recalls his mother never saying a word about his efforts to do something as simple—but unusual for Blacks—as getting a library card in downtown Troy, Alabama. It was 1956, and Lewis was sixteen. However, his mother took a different approach, by way of a letter to him. She was concerned that his efforts to shake up the seemingly impenetrable racist system of inequality in this country would get him killed. Lewis remembers his mother was very uneasy with his attempts to become the first Black to attend Troy State University. His mother was afraid that as a consequence of his actions, her house would be bombed or burned. They could lose their land. The family might be relentlessly harassed. These were very real concerns that even Dr. Martin Luther King Jr. warned the young John Lewis about. He would have been the first Black student to attend that college. But understanding what was at stake and taking into account his mother's concerns, "I dropped the whole idea of going to Troy State."

But Lewis did continue to fight against the racial wrongs in this country, and as a result, his mother's concerns for him continued to grow. But there was a drastic change in her demeanor and conversations when Lewis helped to bring about the Civil Rights Act of 1964 and the Voting Rights Act of 1965. Lewis says his mother was more "proud and pleased once she realized that she had the right to vote." And this was thanks to her son's efforts (and the efforts of thousands like him). She became an activist in her own right and made it her mission to register other Blacks to vote.

So as we look at what our men say about race to our sons, I want to explore the opposite side of the parental conversation. What does *mama* say about race to her sons and daughters? In the Black community, the mother holds our families together, and she is the one, in most cases, who spends the most time with the children. Our mothers are our first teachers. I remember the wisdom of my mother on race. I learned early on, especially as I watched those old black-and-white movies, falling in love with the hero, who was usually White and whose screen persona spoke negative things about Blacks. My mother was quick to point out that everyone was not as embracing of our community as I imagined it was in the movies.

★ ★ ★

The week of June 22, 2015, was a huge week in Washington and across the United States. Race dominated the international landscape. I was in London with my children, wanting to expose them to a different culture and give them more life chances, just as my mother did for me. I was on a promotional tour for my first book, *The Presidency in Black and White*, and it also happened to be my older daughter's thirteenth birthday. While in London, I met with members of Parliament from the House of Commons and the House of Lords. The overriding theme was strong support for President Obama. But there was a general consensus of pessimism when it came to fixing the race problems in the United States. It occurred to me that London, being such a multicultural international city, sees itself as more accepting racially than we are in the United States. Yes, they have their problems, but not on the scale of America. The Brits called out Baltimore, Charleston, New York, and Ferguson as if these events were in their own country. But what happened that same week, just across the pond in the United States, resounded more than we could ever imagine.

In June 2015, we heard America's first Black president say the word *nigger* in an interview for a popular podcast. The next day the governor of the state of South Carolina and the head of the Republican National Committee (RNC) said that it was time to take down the Confederate flag. Reince Priebus, the head of the RNC, even went so far as to say, "We are a country more united than we are divided." Then, later that week, President Obama delivered his most stirring and truthful talk to the nation on race at the funeral of Mother Emanuel Church's Pastor Clementa Pinckney, who had been assassinated a few days earlier in a racially motivated mass slaying. The president gave a soaring speech of a better day and God's amazing grace as we are a country still divided along racial lines. He pushed the envelope for some when he said "Johnnie" will get the callback and "Jamal" won't. It was a week of amazing triumph in the midst of tremendous hurt.

Just a few months prior, the spotlight was on poverty in my hometown of Baltimore. Former Mayor Kurt Schmoke said Baltimore is a "tale of two cities" that focuses on income. When you drill down on income, it breaks down to race. At that time, as a mother, I had to tell my two daughters about the harsh realities of life in America, and that reality was so close to home, almost in our backyard, as the Baltimore riots catapulted the city into the race debate.

Ryan's and Grace's America had, thus far, been pure and sweet. I had wanted them to be sugar and spice and everything nice, but the reality they were facing was far different. My two daughters attended a predominantly White, wealthy, all-girls school in the Baltimore area. They mingled with extreme privilege and impressive academic scholarship awardees at the school, which was over one hundred years old.

However, the girls were watching national news coverage of local streets and familiar places where we often shopped. Many of those places were ones I cherished from childhood, including the Mondawmin Mall, which was not far from the New Shiloh Baptist Church. The church was the initial point of the rock throwing that took place on April 27, 2015, and the site of the Freddie Gray funeral.

I live in Baltimore County, and I am a product of the city. I was raised in Northwest and Northeast Baltimore, growing up and then moving into Baltimore County as a teen. But a harsh visual that was personal on levels of race and community was emerging. I had to face the fact that I must tell my children about the very thing I had hoped to shield them from—the ugly truth about racial inequality in this country. Not only was I forced to have the "talk," but I had to do it as news of riots blared from the TV, car radio, social media, and every other possible outlet. There was no escaping the scary images occurring in places we frequented.

My younger daughter, Grace, was terrified of what she saw on TV, fearing that they would come for us since we were not far away from the chaos. My older daughter, Ryan, had the maturity to put it into perspective and take it in stride. Regardless of their reactions, I knew I had to look calm and seem unafraid to ensure that they felt as safe as possible, since first and foremost, that is my job as a mother. I reassured them that they did not have to worry, because the rioters would not come to us. I would make sure of that! But the day after the riots, schools in our area, businesses, doctor's offices, food stores, and restaurants were closed early because of reports that the rioters would return, this time to our area. The subways were delayed or closed entirely; thus, the riots had left behind something much more dangerous than property destruction—fear.

Maryland State Police helicopters constantly patrolled from the air, getting a bird's-eye view of the destruction below. While the disruption had indeed subsided, the atmosphere was heavy with unrest and uncertainty. The school that my children attended, along with other school systems, took safety precautions by closing early. I didn't go to work at the White House that day, remaining at home on guard as a precaution. I wanted to make sure I wouldn't be trapped in traffic on that two-hour, fifty-mile trek each way from the White House to my home, away from the girls. No one seemed to know what would happen next. After I picked up the girls from school, I decided to stop and get some food, just in case we had to hunker down in the house for the duration. We didn't know what the next few days held for us.

We live in a racially mixed section of our neighborhood that has a large portion of African Americans. Driving home from school with the girls, I saw, along with many others who were trying to get home, a red off-road Ford pickup truck driving erratically in a large strip-mall parking lot that was a bit of a complicated maze. The truck cab, stuffed with four White people, was driving around the lot brandishing two flags. One was a flag with a coiled snake saying "Don't tread on me," and the other one was the South Carolina state flag . . . the Confederate flag.

Needless to say, many of the Black people in their cars looked at one another and probably like me said, "Is that what I think it is? A Confederate flag?" I honestly could not believe my eyes.

As a reporter, I had to get up close and see for myself. I began taking pictures of the truck as I approached, causing my older daughter to question me as to why I was following this truck. I told her about the hate this flag represents to many people. She began to cry and told me to go home, but my reporter instincts were unstoppable. I was cautious but determined. I think the truck driver knew I was taking pictures and trying to get his license plate number. He began to drive fast to elude me. In the end, he got away. This was not the time or the place for this kind of insane behavior, particularly when emotions were already raw.

Yes, we have a right to freedom of expression and freedom of speech. The only problem is, their obviously provocative act in that Black community on that day could have caused a reaction that they were not prepared for. They were metaphorically throwing gasoline on a roaring fire. So as I gave my daughters a bit of history of the evils of the Confederate flag, I also had to tell them a bit more about racism. Later that day, a simple explanation was not enough. I had to go deeper. Think about it! We look at stories, starting from the arrival of Blacks in America, enslaved. It's an ugly series of tales filled with hate and death. But for children, we have to pepper that conversation with hope and brighter days. We have worked hard to be able to provide this very important aspect for our children's lives—hope.

A year earlier, during the summer of 2014, I had touched on race issues with my girls. I remember it vividly because it involved something so simple, but now so threatening, for a Black child's life—my kids' love of their soft-tipped archery and hand cannon sets. My younger daughter went outside to play with her launcher in our private, large, open-spaced backyard. In our neighborhood, all of the yards adjoin each other, with no gates or fences except for a few neighbors' homes. So Grace was in the backyard playing with her toy, as kids do. My aunt happened to be over, and seeing what was going on, she ran outside, telling my six-year-old to come back in immediately! My daughter was shocked and could not understand why she was told to put her toy away. She didn't think she had done anything wrong, but she felt like she had.

Well, Aunt Pearl, my mother's sister, who had been watching my kids for twelve years, told Grace never to play with that toy cannon again outside, because a little boy had been killed recently in Cleveland, Ohio, playing with a toy gun very similar to hers. So when I came home, Grace was still in shock and asked me if that story was true. Sadly, I admitted it was, saying, "Yes." Then I had to show her the online video of the fatal police-involved shooting of Tamir Rice because it seemed so unbelievable for a child as well as for adults to understand. Witnessing it was the only way for her to truly believe such a thing had really happened.

Times have changed, and I didn't want to set the stage for any of that to happen in my home. This is a sad reality many African Americans have to face. Aunt Pearl was concerned that with the growing unrest in the area, someone might get the wrong idea about my daughter's toy. Unfortunately, reality had hit our family with a powerful blow!

The race equation is such a complicated one on so many levels. For example, take the night of February 5, 2015. It was a night of celebration, as I had begun my book tour with a major stop, the Enoch Pratt Free Library in downtown Baltimore. It is one of the "must stops" for any published author. That night was amazing! Baltimore showed up *en masse* to support one of its own. Former Mayor Kurt Schmoke was there, along with some of Baltimore's elite, including the sponsors of the event, Eddie and Sylvia Brown. Also, there was a host of Black female judges from the City of Baltimore. After the event, I was interviewed by a local reporter about the book, and then a group of us traveled to a local hot spot, Tio Pepe, a Mexican restaurant, to eat. (By the way, we ended up shutting that place down!)

There were at least twenty-one professional women gathered together after the event, including a Black female school board member, the youngest in the history of the city. These women were taking me out to celebrate my success. I was so excited to hear what they had to say, and that they wanted to celebrate me. I heard the judges' talk of how they consider themselves a version of a social worker when they are on the bench, listening to challenging cases every day. I heard the pride in the women talking of the school board member, and how she handled her job as the youngest to ever serve. Then they came to *me*, asking *me* about my job and my first book.

It was a wonderful evening. And we wanted to top it off with a picture to remember the event. We all assembled in a large open space near the entrance to the restaurant. Here we were, well-dressed Black women professionals huddled up together just inside the restaurant entrance to take a picture of this amazing gathering. Just then, two fur coat-slinging White women approached us, and one of them said, "Hey, we can't even get by the staff!"

I went ballistic! "Don't you know we are not 'the help'? These are judges and elected officials." Others in my group said, "And she is a White House correspondent and author. How insulting!" They knew we were mad as they tried to step out of the restaurant into the frigid cold. The chill that had swept through the room from their ignorance was worse than the bitter temperature we were about to face outside. Those White women smirked when they heard our disdain for their comments, and their husbands had a perplexed look that also revealed a bit of fear—not knowing if there was going to be an uprising. I am constantly amazed by such ignorance and rudeness!

What those judgmental women saw was a group of Black women, and they immediately assumed we were staff—that was not the slight. The honest work of food workers and those in customer service is as admirable as any other. It was the fact that they were trying to insinuate that we were somehow beneath them, that we couldn't possibly be their equals, or even their superiors. Their contempt was obvious through their sly, slimy smiles. I am far from a violent person, but if ever there was a time I wanted to lay hands on someone, it was that night. My anger and hurt were very real.

With this pervasive arrogance in communities across this nation, among people of all walks of life and varying economic backgrounds, it is not surprising that Baltimore erupted on April 27, 2015, immediately following the Freddie Gray funeral. Young Black kids from the local public schools wanted to show their dismay at a system that was failing them with each shocking headline and news story. They held—what rioters often feel is their only option—a purge.

So with the issue of race rearing its ugly, ever-present head on such a frequent basis, it's time that we perform a deep dive and examine just what is going on and why it continues, despite our perceived collective "evolution" in this modern age. That's exactly why I decided that we need to start at the beginning, start from our first source of education. It's our mothers who may hold the key to unlocking this mystery of how to move past these harmful racial issues.

And, of course, because of my profession and my view of the political atmosphere at the White House, I decided to start at the top and talk with President Barack Obama. Once he leaves office, we will surely look at life as "post-Obama" instead of "postracial." So in a conversation that included four other Black journalists, I asked our commander-in-chief the first question as we traveled in Air Force One, high above the racial chaos that is infecting our cities. Here in the presidential plane's conference room, I was ready to get the conversation started.

March 7, 2015—Aboard Air Force One

APRIL RYAN: Okay, Mr. President, as we look at issues of race, this has been a very historic window these last couple of weeks. Reflecting on these last couple of weeks and then moving forward, there are markers in history. We have one marker that could be Abraham Lincoln with the Emancipation Proclamation. We have LBJ with civil rights and voting rights. And then people say another marker is you. They talk about postracial America. Is this postracial, or would you say post-Obama? Because you have created—effectuated—a lot of change in your administration with criminal justice reform and civil rights issues. Would you say that—would you embrace the idea of a post-Obama or postracial society?

THE PRESIDENT: I'm not sure exactly what you mean by the postracial versus post-Obama, but here's what I—

APRIL RYAN: You being a marker.

THE PRESIDENT: Well, here's what I'll say. I think that there's no doubt that my election was a significant moment in the country's racial history. I say that with all humility. If it hadn't been me, it would have been somebody else. But a barrier was broken.

I think that legacy will continue in the minds of children who are growing up never having known to this point a president who was Black. And I think that shapes attitudes among young African American children, but also among all children. And I'd like to think that that will have a useful, lasting effect in terms of people's attitudes about who can do what, and changes people's images of what's possible for any child in America.

I wouldn't equate my election with seminal moments like the Emancipation Proclamation or the passage of the Civil Rights Act of '64 or the Voting Rights Act of '65. Those were massive changes in legal status that represented fundamental breaks with America's tragic history, and were the pillars—the 13th Amendment, 14th Amendment, and 15th Amendment— of Civil Rights Acts of the '60s. Those were the—those represented the dismantling of formal discrimination in this country. There's nothing that's going to compare to that.

Moving forward, our work is to build on that work to fine-tune that work where we see formal discrimination or state-sponsored discrimination still occurring. But increasingly, our work has to do with dealing with the ongoing legacy of a divided society—closing the opportunity gaps, closing the achievement gaps, closing the wealth gaps—that inevitably have been passed on from generation to generation because the gaps were so wide.

And that involves no one piece of legislation, but it requires a host of different efforts. It means investing in early childhood education. It means us making sure everybody has health insurance. It means the kind of public-private work that we're doing through My Brother's Keeper. It means getting more African Americans in STEM education, in math and science and engineering.

And so there's not going to be one silver bullet, but rather it's going to be a sustained effort on a variety of fronts that will take us on the next leg of this journey towards a more just society.

Valerie Jarrett, in her office in the White House West Wing in early 2016, during the last year of the Obama administration, acknowledged, "As we have seen, just over the last couple of years in particular, there has been a spotlight on the fact that we still have extraordinary inequity in this country. We still have discrimination and racism that should not come as any surprise. None of us were under any illusion that just by electing an African American president that generations of legacy of racism was going to evaporate overnight."

Looking at both statements, from President Obama and Valerie Jarrett, the inequity and pervasive racial bias globally and here at home is so deep and ingrained in our being as a people that we don't always see with the naked eye, at our first glance, that race is a factor in almost everything we see and do. That explains why, for hundreds of years, people have turned their heads and closed their eyes to this ugly cancer that permeates this country. Racism persists at its worst levels, even today.

· 2 ·

Born a Statistic

"Well-behaved women seldom make history!"

Thank God for whoever coined that phrase! It screams of nonconformity and a move from the rules and standards society places on us as people and particularly as women. It says that no matter what the general mind meld is, we have got to walk in our own destinies. We need to buck the system and dare not to conform to society's ideas of who we are or should be and what box they may want to place us in. This speaks volumes of those who worked and are still working to change the negative stereotypes and negative statistical data that always keep the ball from rolling forward for women and women of color.

The ultimate realization is that in many cases, we must abandon the standards and norms preset for many of us. The gauntlet has been laid down, meaning we are actively engaged in the fight for parity in a society that has yet to fully value women. However, this revolution is a combination fight for skin tone and gender. Make no mistake, this revolution will not, now or ever, be pretty and for the most part will not be televised. The late New York Congresswoman Shirley Chisholm said it best: "If they don't give you a seat at the table, bring a folding chair."

As a kid growing up in the '70s and '80s, history books, mainstream media, and the three major television networks at that time never gave us the full view of the greatness of women and women of color. I am in awe of people like Shirley Chisholm, the first Black woman elected to the US Congress, in 1968. She also took her brand of feminism even higher when she became a Democratic candidate for president in 1972, running on behalf of all people but often speaking of society's concepts and views of women and women of color in very different and real terms, unlike the standard clichés. Chisholm saw "the emotional, sexual, and psychological stereotyping of females begins when the doctor says: It's a girl." And if we add another component, skin color, another statistical stereotype arises. Chisholm also profoundly addressed overcoming the "double whammy of being Black and female."

Ed Towns, a former Brooklyn, New York, congressman, met Chisholm in the 1960s when he was a community activist and she was a New York state assemblyperson. He says affectionately, "Shirley was my lady!" Towns recalls when people would say to her, "You can't do this!" she would find it important to give it a shot. Those public challenges resulted in her run for Congress and, against mighty odds, winning that historic seat. Towns remembers that out of the eight Democratic clubs in her district, only one supported her bid, and the rest is her story.

When Chisholm felt it was time to step down from Congress, after making her indelible mark, she looked for her replacement. It was a man! With all her pioneering work for women, she turned to Brooklyn's first Black deputy borough president, Ed Towns. She called him on the phone while she was in Oklahoma. In her incredible journey, she was able to uplift women, but she was mindful not to diminish men. He realized her revolutionary work was with and for women in this nation. Towns will never forget Chisolm's response to his question about her making this move with a male replacement. She said, "Yes, I am for the women. I am for the women's movement, but I never said that I was not for a good man." Chisholm left Congress in 1983.

Peering back at Chisolm and her revolutionary efforts for women that translated to a fight for the underdog and all of America, the coldness of yesterday's realities persists. And it's more a commentary about the ills humanity allows without a challenge to genderism and racism. Chisholm, a fierce truth teller for all times, found that "In the end, anti-Black, anti-female, and all forms of discrimination are equivalent to the same thing—anti-humanism."

Cornell Belcher, Democratic pollster, supports the Chisholm theory on a broader scale: "I think race in America trumps almost anything. I think there are very few things that race does not trump in America, particularly American politics."

Now let's add another layer to our already-complicated equation. When it comes to women, by our very nature we were born to be overcomers as we lead in our various spaces. But with our greatness, as either the head or a major factor in our households, in 2015 we are still a gender in this modern age physically and mentally absent from chunks of society dominated by White males. The backdrop is the second term and the fourth quarter of the Obama administration, when the Blacklash to the Barack Obama presidency is painfully evident. It is not a typing error. I indeed meant "Blacklash"!

Almost any minority group is now the bull's-eye of a target for the bigotry of some of the presidential candidates, and the foul anti-woman rhetoric spewing from the face of billionaire, and Republican presidential candidate, Donald Trump.

Without singling out parties, it's about not viewing and respecting women as equal players. This ugly fact reared its head in 2012 during the Romney/ Obama face-off for the Oval Office. Women became an unintended focus. There was a pivot off presidential politics onto designating qualified women to fill cabinet positions in Massachusetts when Mitt Romney was governor. Governor Romney had an overwhelming number of male applicants for the posts that needed to be filled, but where were the women? During the October 2012 presidential debate, Romney claimed he reached out to women's groups to find cabinet qualifiers. That's when the groups brought "binders" of qualified women to him. Is it just the fact that only women know of other qualified women and men are oblivious to our accomplishments? I hope that's not true! Even as that political gender staffing controversy is vividly recalled years later, Republican Party Chairman Reince Priebus contends that for society as a whole, "in many cases women are the 24-hour decision makers and the first line of defense."

Not only are we, as women, absent from the radar of the general thought processes, but when it comes to being Black women, we are invisible no matter what heights we have risen to and achieved. We bear the brunt of hurt historically, as we are the glue of the family, the backbone of society, holding everyone up. Yet we as women are not a full part of society—in all aspects. There is a dizzying cycle to this issue in the real world. In 1952 Ralph Waldo Ellison penned the novel *The Invisible Man*, a story of a Black man living in New York City who walked a model life and went "underground," believing his existence was invisible to American society.

Now imagine a true-life story of a Black woman who has achieved the ultimate titanium ring in twenty-first-century Washington, DC. She, one of the most influential and recognizable people of any gender or race, confronted not only the physical condition of being unseen, but she was also in the crosshairs of the racist and jaded mental situation of being unnoticed. An extreme, but very real example, during the Obama administration years, First Lady Michelle Obama would leave the secure bubble of the White House, 1600 Pennsylvania Avenue, her home at the time, to venture out for walks and exercise, fulfilling her personal agenda of her Let's Move campaign. She would walk the streets of Washington, DC, around the White House, unannounced and in most cases unnoticed.

She was rarely recognized, and because of that fact, the unpublicized walks continued. She walked by everyday America: workers, tourists, and residents. But for the most part she took long walks away from the White House without any fanfare from those she encountered along the way. This beautiful and statuesque woman, the wife of the leader of the Free World, was not recognized! This tall, accomplished woman was nearly invisible to all those who unknowingly encountered her during her walks. Valerie Jarrett, Mrs. Obama's friend dating back decades from Chicago, would take these walks with her. Jarrett says this "makes the point what African American women experience every day, so if you don't notice her, you certainly are not going to notice other African American women." Jarrett reminds us how Mrs. Obama has been impactful in her duties as First Lady, mother, and human being, and that has caused everyone to take another look.

Both Jarrett and Mrs. Obama recalled this shocking fact, as they realized they were only noticed by a few people on those walks. Mrs. Obama was not recognized and therefore was rarely bothered by anyone. More importantly, the public didn't pay attention to her most likely because of her race. And for most people, when they look at a person, race is the first thing they see. Michelle Obama, the First Lady of the United States of America, was "invisible," according to Jarrett. This woman, an icon, whose face has graced the cover and front page of every national and international newspaper, magazines as well as on television news programs, entertainment shows, and so on, was now "invisible"! This was in spite of the fact that she had essentially lost the usual animosity because of her husband's meteoric rise to the Oval Office.

That is juxtaposed with former First Lady Laura Bush taking a walk in February 2005 to the Corcoran Art Gallery. She walked there from the southwest side of the White House, just two blocks across the street. But as she was walking, people immediately spotted her and instantly there were clicks of cameras taking pictures, and gasps of disbelief were audible in the air. Yes, she was beautifully dressed, and her makeup was impeccable and meticulously applied. She was escorted by some plainclothes and uniformed Secret Service officers dotting the path, but she was noticed.

I don't care how casual and without makeup Michelle Obama is, she stands out! But the reality is, she is a minority. More specifically, she's a Black woman in America, and the general thought of mainstream America is, she doesn't exist. With all her major accomplishments, the Ivy League schools she has attended, and even being the First Lady of the United States, the folks on the street consigned her to being less than who she is and even *invisible*.

Close your eyes for a minute and look at who Michelle Obama is without making this political. Her pedigree alone is more than impressive. So now I ask you the question. Was she invisible? If so, why? Does someone of color need police protection to make you recognize the status of who they are? Or is it simply that she's Black, and presuppositions prevent humankind from looking deeper into who this person really is? Jarrett says, "Oftentimes I think

African American women are invisible. . . . Oftentimes we are discounted and we are not relevant to some people's frame of reference."

There is depth to the Black woman's relevance issue, as Jarrett finds in her work as head of the President's Initiative on Women and Girls. She believes this point is further perpetuated as some of those in the mainstream "do not have an African American friend, they have never worked with an African American woman, they are not used to seeing an African American woman in leadership positions, and this is the first time they have had an African American First Lady."

So the invisibility issue is not just based on gender but is also compounded with the varying shades of Black skin tones. W. E. B. DuBois wrote in 1903, "The problem of the Twentieth Century is the problem of color line." The US Census Bureau statistics found that in 2014 the population of the United States was 318.9 million. That is a lot of people, but the country is not crowded enough to where bodies are hard to see. What happened to Mrs. Obama realistically is a representation of what many of the twenty-three million Black women in this country face, being unseen. When we speak of being unseen, we are not just speaking of the literal sense. It involves premade concepts that are already embedded in the mind and hard to chisel away.

Historically, the strength of women is in the tales from the centuries, the stories that are passed down from one generation to another in families and communities. Former O. J. Simpson Los Angeles Prosecutor Christopher Darden is well aware of issues of race but was torn when he found out, just years ago, about his mother's encounters with racism. Darden was conflicted about this, as he had never known these stories about his mother. She was eighty-one years old when he had the discussion with her about these life-changing incidents. He remembers writing about race and dealing with matters of race in his profession and never knew about his own mother's experiences. With a bit of hurt in his heart, he cross-examined himself about this revelation. Part of his self-examination included analyzing his mother's skin tone as to why he did not look to her on matters of race.

She was raised by her grandmother, his great-grandmother, a freckle-faced, very light-complexioned Black woman. His mother grew to become a tall, fair, freckle-faced, and shapely woman. Darden remembers as a young child, she was so attractive that his dad would make sure either he or one of their sons would accompany her to town because she caused heads to turn. Darden himself asked, "Did I ignore her [race] experience because I didn't think she would have experienced racism in a meaningful way—like men— because she is a woman or because she is fair?"

Her experiences, like those of the rest of us, mattered. Mrs. Darden raised eight children and was considered a voracious reader, poring over everything, including the classics and Shakespeare. All this she did without finishing high school. She was determined to defy the odds in a racist society, realizing it was an uphill battle. The heavy weight of the odds are constantly pressing, but there is also a constant battle to beat the assumed probability of falling into the pile of alarming statistical figures. Darden said of his mother, "In her years, she found that White people, especially White men, are intimidated by Black people and afraid of the Black man. White men were always afraid Black men might and would catch up to them. So they always kept them down."

During the war and after, Mrs. Darden saw signs that said *Hiring. Colored need not apply.* It hurt her, and it hurt her family. Darden reflects back on their life in California as a family: "Daddy would walk for miles to Richmond and then to San Francisco looking for work, and nobody would hire him. Out of the Army he would get a job washing dishes."

There were consequences in the family during that time when the qualified husband could not find work. Mrs. Darden recalled how it put pressure on her relationship and her family. She recalled many decades before when this was her reality: "A man that cannot feed his family becomes broken!" She saw how they treated a lot of Black men. They were laborers and not much else. Chris Darden said, "Once Daddy got a job as a trash man, picking up trash in those big silver cans and walking out to the truck. Hard, hard work. The boss told my dad one day that he should not quit the trash company because he could go far." Mrs. Darden remembered that the man said, "You're one of the few colored around here that can read and write." Darden says that impacted his mother. "My mother always remembered that. It motivated her to make sure we did well in school. C's were not allowed in my house. Mama said that Black parents have to do better with Black kids. Teach them from the time they are born. Read to them the first day and keep reading to them. Make them go to school. Make them learn. Help your child. If you don't know the material, learn it yourself. Mama said she would go the library to make sure she knew what we were learning so she could help us study."

Mrs. Darden sits back in her evening years and sees the work she and her husband poured into their children when they were not allowed to be more themselves. Not all of her eight kids attended college, but four did—two at UC Berkeley, one at Dartmouth, and one became a lawyer. And another is a police officer.

Even with yesterday's often-unheralded victories by Black women, we remain stuck in a cycle of a different kind of oppression: a lack of opportunity. The Center for American Progress issued some distressing findings. These findings are from their report "Women of Color and the Gender Wage Gap," released online April 14, 2015. It states:

> Across the board, women of color are more likely than white women to
> be shunted into the lowest-earning occupations in the service sector and

in sales and office jobs. This trend is particularly pronounced for Hispanic women. Among working women in 2014, 62 percent of Hispanics were clustered into just two job groups—service occupations and sales and office occupations. This is compared with 57 percent of blacks, 51 percent of whites, and 44 percent of Asians in the same job categories.

In 2014, only 35 percent of black women and 26 percent of Hispanic women were employed in higher-paying management, professional, and related jobs—compared with 48 percent of Asian women and 43 percent of white women. While one could argue that women of color choose to work in lower-paying service-sector occupations, it is hard to discount the fact that women of color often enter the labor force with significant barriers to success. African American and Hispanic women are significantly less likely to graduate from high school or to get a bachelor's degree than white women. This places African American and Hispanic women at a disadvantage from the moment they enter the workforce, creating major structural barriers to entering top-earning professional fields.

What compounds the harsh truth revealed by the Center for American Progress is that Black women make 64 cents for every dollar a White man makes, and Hispanic women make 54 cents for every dollar earned by White men. The truth to these stats shows poverty is not far away for the least of these in this society. The state of women, particularly Black women, is stark. Valerie Jarrett told *Essence* magazine in its September 2015 issue:

> Forty [percent] of working mothers are now the sole or primary bread winners, and 55% of African-American families are headed by a single mother—compared with 21% of White households. Women still earn 77 cents on the dollar compared with men, and African-American women earn just 64 cents on the dollar compared with men.

And if we are really being honest with ourselves, many of these women in these stats are living in poverty. There is more jaw-dropping evidence from the Center for Global Policy Solutions. In their 2016 release, "The Racial Wealth Gap," they state that:

> When it comes to the Wealth Gap and Women of Color, in 2007, White women had a median wealth of $45,400, compared to $100 and $120 respectively for African American and Latina women. The Study also finds when it comes to the overall African American Wealth Gap the median wealth of White households is 20 times that of African American households. African Americans are almost three times less likely to have a bank account compared to the general population. Only 44 percent of African Americans own a home compared to 73.5 percent of Whites.

As you see, we have statistics everywhere, but the problems still persist. Race and gender are factors when it comes to the bottom rung of the economic chain. The devil is in the details. New Jersey Senator Cory Booker says it is not the fault of women for falling into the statistical heap. "We focus the attention in the wrong place. Everybody wants to lecture single moms about what to do when the lecturing should be to us, as in the greater community. It is ridiculous to me that there is not a network raising our kids anymore and that single moms are facing increasing challenges; it is all on them. We are the only industrialized country in the world that doesn't have paid family leave. I talk to moms who have to make these terrible decisions. Their child has asthma and they're missing school being rushed to the hospital. That parent has to miss work; that means missing that paycheck, missing their ability to keep their family afloat. We put horrible pressures on women now and think they are the problem. The problem is our society."

From his immaculately kept Capitol Hill Senate office, Booker lifts up women for accomplishing all they have as they are working against terrible odds. "It is extraordinary how women have been playing such a strong central role in Black culture for as long as I have known it, especially in environments where Black men have seen incredible challenges. It has created a reality where so many Black women have to step up and do everything."

Black women are often the leader in the home and community as the senator also referenced in *The New York Times* article (April 20, 2015), "1.5 Million Missing Black Men" by Justin Wolfers, David Leonhardt, and Kevin Quealy. Booker believes the missing Black male in our society is one of the contributing factors to the challenges faced by Black women.

Booker made the statements to me during our interview, with poignant pictures and figurines of the civil rights struggle for equality in this country as our witnesses.

Delving deeper into the issue of Black women, Senator Booker acknowledged his father was "born to a single mother, born poor." When she was having trouble taking care of him, "It was another family that helped raise my dad, stepped up into the gap." Nonetheless, as his grandmother was a statistic, he sees the grace in the effort to survive the uphill journey.

Other stats get worse, this time for missing women. According to a *Boston Review* article, "The Invisibility of Black Women," by Christopher Lebron, that appeared on January 15, 2015,

> There is the horrific fact that more than sixty thousand black women are missing in America. To put that number into perspective, black women make up roughly 8 percent of the population in the United States but

nearly 37 percent of missing women. The explanation for the missing women is often unclear; it includes the typical suspects: murder, running away, abduction, and so on. But it is clear that there are at least two problems having to do with our treatment of this full-blown crisis. First, the media tends to publicize stories of missing white women or girls so much more than it does stories of missing women of color that there is a term for it: Missing White Woman Syndrome. Second, what little bandwidth the media does have for missing black people tends to be filled with discussion of the American shame of mass incarceration, which disproportionately affects black men, cast as a metaphorical "missing." While that phenomenon is a travesty and deserving of all the attention it receives and more, the concurrent absence of media coverage about the epidemic of missing black women renders them doubly invisible: gone and seemingly forgotten.

The Black mother who was labeled a hero after being featured in a viral video slapping her son during the Baltimore riot of 2015 received a lot of feedback from the community.

Senator Cory Booker contends, "We need to stop beating up on that single mother as the circumstances around her contribute to her plight. It is not hers alone."

Valerie Jarrett responds in the affirmative to Booker's statement, confirming, "Black women are the backbone of our community. When you think about what Black women have been up against in this country, many times raising their children on their own, trying to provide a protective, safe environment in the middle of chaos for their kids. I mean, I will tell you in Chicago, having spent a lot of time working in public housing and you see how every time when they send their children to school, they don't know if they are going to come home, when they are going to school across the courtyard from each other, living in fear every single day and yet helping their children every day achieve over enormous odds. There is a lot to be said for the Black woman in America."

Even as stats have a dim offering on the state of Black women, there are Black women who every day are silently making things work for their families and unknowingly moving the ball forward for others. Senator Booker's mother, Caroline Jordan Booker, born Caroline Jordan in December 1939, "has had an extraordinary career," according to her son. Booker, beaming with pride in his office a few weeks before Christmas in 2015, says she was an "incredible trailblazer" in corporate America. She was one of IBM's early African American hires and rose to an executive-level post where "she helped with diversity issues in human resources" matters at the giant tech company. Senator Booker says of her example, "She has been my role model all my life."

The junior senator from New Jersey feels deeply that his mother has done incredible things in her life, always serving others. "I witnessed her always being a servant, leading organizations from the Fair Housing Council, to the Urban League, to running at one point a homeless organization in Atlanta. The older I get the more I appreciate how much of a super woman she really is. Somebody who can really be raising my brother and me, along with my dad. Very present all the time in my life from sporting events to parent and teacher conferences to when I got sick as well as being a corporate executive and being successful in her career there. And importantly, modeling for me service. Always about giving back to others and being there for folks paying forward all the blessings she had.

"When I was a young kid—just born—I was a baby. My parents moved into the town I grew up in. My parents in many ways had to fight a civil rights battle just to move into the town, Harrington Park, New Jersey. Real estate agents weren't showing them homes in White neighborhoods. They were steering them (away)."

The Booker family was in the midst of housing discrimination. In the 1920s through the 1940s, there were racially "restrictive covenants" that prevented people of color from purchasing homes in White communities. Meanwhile, the fight was on for the Booker family to move to the community. Booker says, "It was an extraordinary place to grow up. But my parents went to the Fair Housing Council. They used a White couple to pose as my parents, to put a down payment—to put a bid on the house. The bid was accepted. Contracts were drawn up. On the day of the closing, the White couple did not show up, my father did, and a volunteer Fair Housing Council lawyer. And a fight broke out where the real estate agent attacked my father's lawyer."

Also of that encounter, Senator Booker said, "They sicced the dog on my dad . . . and it turned out to be a big, almost legal battle. Eventually we moved in as the first Black family in the segregated town—in that segregated town. So I always had a mom that was breaking barriers. She graduated from Fisk University and really began, especially through IBM, helping to integrate a company, then moving into a town, helping to integrate a town. But she never lost her roots and her connection, whether it was through her sorority, through the links, through so many organizations that she was involved in, always understanding she could not pay back all the blessings that were given to her. She had to pay them forward and raise my brother and I to understand that we are blessed with abundance from where we were growing up compared to where my mom and dad grew up. But these blessings should not be luxuriated in, but they should be metabolized as fuel for us to continue to fight for greater equality and opportunity in America."

Black women can't be ignored, despite the omission of their physical condition in history books or the small acknowledgments of their lives with a few paragraphs in books and magazines about their existence. The impact of Black women on this nation resounds! Centuries ago, Harriet Tubman, soon to grace the US $20 bill, fiercely and secretively helped thousands escape to freedom. She and others made hundreds of successful runs from the South to the North through the woods, and using waterways, with help from the Underground Railroad. Those trips were ultimately costly for the White landowners. They lost some of their free labor. Tubman's cunning translated into White men searching her out. She was far from invisible; she was just the opposite, very much wanted. They wanted to find her, to stop her, tear her down, and even kill her. But Tubman's spirit could not be chained or broken. She is quoted as saying, "I freed a thousand slaves. I could have freed a thousand more if only they knew they were slaves."

As she pushed for freedom, her approach was primitive, but there was a definite sophistication in the end result. Tubman, not formally educated, but learned, said, "I grew up like a neglected weed—ignorant of liberty, having no experience of it." However, at that time, liberty of some sort was what the thousands she led north embraced. She is Booker's favorite American hero and he said, "God gave her freedom. She escaped. She was free!" Her life's work, a ministry of freedom, makes the New Jersey senator believe, "We have got to be in the struggle." He reflects on the meaning of words in a song by the musical group Sweet Honey in the Rock, "We who believe in freedom cannot rest."

Booker looks at the issues of race, justice, and challenges with a clear-eyed view from the perspective of history and the fight that continues. "I just think the spirit of African American women continuing to do the kind of things that Harriet Tubman did, Ella Baker did, Madam C. J. Walker, Mary McLeod Bethune—I think that tradition is still alive and well, even as the visuals from the media are negative and stereotypical, that part is a 'bias,' 'perversion,' 'falsehood,' and a tired trope that is not my experience."

In his twenties, future Senator Cory Booker spent his professional career where he "came of age," in Newark, New Jersey. His truth was that he was surrounded by "a tradition of extraordinary Black women" that he experienced in his family and in Newark. These new mother figures, an extended new family for him, held up the citizenry. They were the tenant head of his building and the community leaders, who were given the unofficial yet official titles as "mothers of the community."

Georgia congressman and former head of the Student Nonviolent Coordinating Committee (SNCC) John Lewis reflects on the unbelievable women who worked to help lift the plight of Blacks in this country. He remembers Fannie Lou Hamer, saying she was "wonderful" and an "extraordinary" person. Ella Baker was like the mother of SNCC. He also remembers, "There are so many untold stories. But women in the movement never received their rightful due in the role they played. Even in the sit-ins, Diane Nash, who had been a student at Howard and transferred to Fisk and became one of the real leaders of the student movement, as did Gloria Richardson, who was a mother."

When we look at Black mothers, just as people of color, we should not view them as a monolith. For me, motherhood is personal. I look to my mother, who, from the beginning, taught me about the intricate matters of race and wanted me to understand how those dynamics play out daily in our lives, in ways seen and unseen. She nurtured me from the moment she conceived me to her last breath of life. Mary Vivian Gowans Ryan died May 2007, the year I turned forty. It was the same year my last child was born. She left an indelible mark on my life, and her influence on me is still very real and evident. My mother's influence has made me look at how she raised me and exposed me to things to encourage me to be better and do better in life. I look at the similarities and not-so-obvious likenesses of the mothering both my mother and I gave to our children.

Peering into who I am as a mother in an urban community, I am a person who looks at life practically. I am the head of a household and the single breadwinner of my home, covering three of us, our dog and our five fish. It is definitely not easy on so many levels, but I keep trying, like so many other women out there. I am a divorced mother raising two children, fourteen and nine, without the physical or emotional help of my ex-husband. I can't help but think of those reflections of me: single and/ or divorced mothers doing their best to make it. They are my *sheroes*! It's not easy, especially when the fathers of our children don't help when they can and should. But when we see statistics, realistically many of us are in that number.

I am a statistic even though I came from a middle-class family unit, where my parents stayed together until death separated them. I am a statistic even though I work at the White House, at the seat of world power. And I am a statistic, even though years ago, as I thought about crafting my life, I thought that divorced status would not be me. I deeply hoped to be married until an old age or until death did us part. Neither was the case.

The Bureau of Labor Statistics, in its October 2013 study, "Marriage and Divorce Patterns by Gender, Race and Educational Attainment," found that "Approximately 43% of marriages that took place at ages 15–46 ended in divorce." The study also found that "On average, women married at younger ages than men. Compared with Whites and Hispanics, Blacks were less likely to marry and conditional on marriage more likely to divorce."

When I began working at the White House, I made a strong connection with someone I did not know was more like me than I realized. That connection was being a divorced mother working hard to keep it together for the sake of our children. I was surprised to learn so many people knew my struggle. I was ultimately told by Valerie Jarrett that President Obama respected me a lot because of how I worked hard and that I was a single parent of two small children, working at the White House daily, and reporting and trying to make a living for my girls 50 miles away in Baltimore. No, it is not easy, but I did not know he really saw that in me. I remember then-President George W. Bush saying something to me about, yes, I was a reporter, but what he saw first was that I was a mother.

Well, in the first term of the Obama administration, I forged a relationship with Jarrett. She was Senior Advisor to President Obama and the head of the White House Council for Women and Girls. She was mentoring many young women about single motherhood. Her discussions with them went far beyond her capacity at the White House. They were much more intimate and personal. Jarrett grew up in privilege; yet in her early adulthood, thirty years ago, she experienced the hard knocks of being a divorced mother. Her privilege did not shield her from what being a single mom entailed.

Her story is very interesting, and I am so thankful and honored she shared her experiences with me. As a young girl, she lived a life of affluence in Chicago, where she was part of a nuclear family with a mother and father in the home together. She has said, with gratitude, that her parents loved her "unconditionally," "invested in her unselfishly," and "set high expectations" for her. They were never concerned about what she would do when she grew up. They gave her the understanding that she would become someone of significance, with all that had been poured into her life. Jarrett says, "My life was far easier than many people I know!" Her father was the first African American to receive tenure at the University of Chicago School of Medicine and her mother was an educator.

Jarrett was fortunate to have a great education. She was a kid whose parents paid for her school tuition without asking for or needing financial aid. Jarrett remembers that "unlike many of my colleagues I went to school with," and those she worked with at the White House, she never had to worry about "financial aid and student loans and student debt." With all of life's blessings, and her efforts to give back to the community, and working in the White House, and being the closest advisor to President Obama, she ended up being a statistic. According to society and its norms, no matter what your pedigree or background, the harsh reality is that when you are raising a child or children alone, society immediately places you in a certain category. However, Jarrett refutes her status as a statistic, saying, "I think I was a pretty good mom and I think there are a lot of ways those statistics can cut."

Jarrett is from affluence and a family of firsts. Her great-grandfather Robert Robinson Taylor was accepted into MIT, becoming its first African American graduate. He was the first professionally trained African American architect.

Booker T. Washington hired him to design and expand the Tuskegee Institute in Alabama. And her grandfather, Robert Rochon Taylor, became the first African American to be named the head of the Chicago Housing Authority. Her mother, Barbara Taylor Bowman, an expert in early childhood development, was the founder of the Erikson Institute and acclaimed for her work in early childhood development. Her father, Dr. James E. Bowman, a renowned pathologist and geneticist, was the first African American resident at Chicago's St. Luke's Hospital.

Jarrett has used her life as an example for women to know that things may be hard now, but understand there is hope. She admits that talking about your personal life in this way is not an easy subject, and it can be uncomfortable. But Jarrett uses her life to show others they can make it and as well help others along the way. Jarrett was briefly married and had a beautiful baby girl over thirty years ago. When her daughter was seven months old, her husband took a job in the medical field in another community, far away. Valerie stayed in Chicago with her child and essentially became a single mom, raising her child alone. Clearly not a fan of the word "statistic," Jarrett reflects, saying, "It may have been harder for me than women who weren't single moms, but my daughter turned out okay!"

Jarrett's husband left a wife and a baby, and she wondered, "How did this happen?" She clearly had not planned this. Her parents and her then-husband's parents had been friends for decades, and this was not part of the plan. Her parents and her husband's parents had stayed married, and she had "married the boy next door." The family connections were even stronger, going back to their grandmothers being best friends. You would think the family connections and the stability of the marriages of the parents would foster a beautiful fairy tale, like the ones this society loves to promote and make movies about. But they didn't!

It was the exact opposite for Valerie Jarrett as they were "supposed to be," at the beginnings of her adult life. "To swim against that current took a lot for me!" Her married life changed as her husband's residency took him to Pontiac, Michigan. But with the realities of life as they were, she was left to raise her child alone. Over thirty years ago, the stigma of divorce was worse than it is today. But for Jarrett it was all about "resilience," "determination," "the courage to look within yourself" and take "the gut check we need from time to time and to decide that no matter what your circumstances are, we have a lot more in our control than we sometimes may think."

VJ, as she is called around the White House, contends that support was what made the difference, and she says all of us, no matter the situation, when it all boils down to it, we are all the same. "Work with the hand you are dealt!" VJ's parents were both "pulling for her" to make it. Her support included her father picking her daughter up from school daily, never missing a day. She said that support from her parents made all the difference. It was "the fortitude I needed when things got tougher!" When it comes to other single mothers, "There are a lot of single mothers out there who raise their children amazingly with far less support than I had. Just because you are a single mom does not mean your child is worse off!"

I honestly think my link to Valerie Jarrett as a friend began because of her keen understanding of being a divorced parent like me. We both shared in different ways our unique ups and downs. There was a common thread. Mine was by way of being the custodial parent for two girls, without help with day-to-day issues like transportation to school, doctors, or anything else. Once I understood Valerie's story, I could see the commonality in our circumstances as different but the same.

But what stats about single motherhood don't tell you is about the "resilience and determination" needed to change the perceived dynamic of that condition. Jarrett in her West Wing office, adorned with snapshots of her life, including photos of friends and family and her times with President Obama and the Obama family, has said, "Do I wish that she [her daughter] had a father in her life? Sure I do! But I used to tell her, as I am sure you do with your children, 'if you've got one parent who loves you, that's more than most people have. Cause some people have two parents, they're not both good, or neither of them are good.' Every child needs someone pulling for them."

Jarrett says that some of her work on the White House Council for Women and Girls was an effort to help foster support for those women who did not have help like she did. She felt, "How can we make life easier for them?"

Peering deeper into the stats and who may fall into statistical categories, if we really look at them, many of us would be considered a statistic. As I've said, I'm a statistic, a divorced mother of two girls. It's mentally painful considering myself a stat, viewed by society as a whole in the worst light. My "well-thought-out" choices led me to this situation. But am I really a statistic? I'm raising two kids as the custodial parent and sending them to a private school that is a feeder school for Ivy League universities.

Reverend Iyanla Vanzant holds similar attitudes about the issue of being a statistic. Vanzant said, "When I was on public assistance, I was not a welfare mother. Because for me those were states of consciousness and the labels that people put on you to hold you to their standards and criteria. If you show up looking like, acting like, thinking like, they think about you, you cannot expect them to treat you differently. And I didn't expect to be treated like a welfare mother. I did not expect to be treated like a woman who had children without a partner. I never called myself a single mother. Ever! I was never a single mother. You know why? I had other women in my community help me raise my children. I had a grandmother who was there for me. I wasn't single. I was unpartnered. That is a different definition. I was never a statistic. I don't care who was counting."

No matter the stats, Jarrett finds hope, even in the bleak numbers for people of color. President Obama and the First Lady are beacons. So when First Lady Michelle Obama sat down with some high school girls, she talked about what it was like to go to public high school in Chicago and have never heard of Princeton, and she said that the only reason she had heard of it is because her brother, Craig, played basketball there. She also talked about a college counselor telling her she couldn't possibly get into a good school. But yet she applied, succeeded, did well, and went on to graduate school at Harvard. She is such a positive role model!

During her last months at the White House, Jarrett confided to me, "One of my favorite phrases lately is, 'There is no better revenge than success.'"

Her parents gave her the formula of perceived success in this country when it came to being Black and female. Jarrett said like many other Black parents in this country, who had to work extra hard just for the basics of life, "My parents said to me when I was younger, 'Yeah, you are going to have to work twice as hard, yeah you are, deal with it. You're going to have to deal with it because of your race, your sex. Life isn't going to be easy; it is going to be really hard. But if you commit to just really working hard at it and trying to keep an optimistic spirit and try to do the very best you can, good things can happen to you. And it doesn't mean there aren't people who deserve a chance. . . .'" She says on matters of equity, "But we have to keep trying."

Trying is right! We must work to change the concepts of other people and the labels they place on us. In some instances we will also have to change the mind-set that we are less than others. That's just not true!

I want to drive home the point that no matter the numbers or categories they place us in, they are not the truth we walk in. From their birth, I have called both my daughters "Princess." That word was challenged by a little White girl at my daughter's preschool. She told my child she was not a princess! This crushed Ryan. Of course she came home and told me what was said to her. I was fortunately able to say "Good-bye!" to my daughter at the school the next day and offered the same farewell I gave her daily, "Good-bye, Princess!" The little White girl looked up at me and said, "Is she a princess?" I said, "Sure," because in that child's mind a Black child couldn't be a princess.

Later on, I had a different experience with Ryan and my other daughter, Grace. In June 2015, I was fortunate to travel to London for a book tour with my girls, my agent, and our team. We toured London and saw Buckingham

Palace, and I told Ryan and Grace, "You are now bona fide princesses, as this is the place where they dub royalty."

These stories are part of the proof that almost anyone can start out in, or at some point in their life fall into, a statistical box. But that doesn't define the person who they ultimately become. For all intents and purposes, I am a statistic. I came from a two-parent home with a married mother and father who split only when the ugly hand of death intruded. I wanted and hoped for that same marital status in my adult life, but I was not able to last in my marriage. The blessing out of the bad situation is my two beautiful girls. I, a divorced mother of two children, I am a statistic. But let's fill out that picture. I am a self-sustaining, divorced, Black woman, not asking the government for anything. I also happen to work 150 feet from *the* seat of power, *world power.*

No matter what twists and turns life brings my girls, they will always know they are more than what society and a numbers cruncher may put on the value of their lives.

• 3 •

A Mother's Love

I am a woman who grew up as a kid in Baltimore with one foot in every social-economic group of the town. I lived in a working-class community, and attended Catholic schools with students from diverse middle-income working-class families. I attended church and I traveled to a hair salon in the hood. My shopping experience was in both the high-end and middle-income stores. But above all my mother exposed me to culture, the fine arts, and education. But in April 2015, the Baltimore I grew up loving was turned upside down. The riots struck a sensitive nerve I did not know was there. I am so close to it but yet so far. I remember driving back from the White House that April evening frantic to get home to my children, Ryan and Grace, not knowing what was going to happen in my community. We were close enough, in the next jurisdiction over from Baltimore City, but miles away. As my heart raced and tears streamed, I was fearful of the unimaginable possibilities of what I could and/or would face when I reached my intended destination. I was constantly on the phone making and receiving calls from family and friends updating me on the situation and inquiring about how I was going to get my children. Fear, hurt, anger, and yes, understanding filled my heart. Where I live stores, schools, doctors' offices, everything was closing down early. I could see and hear helicopters and police cars everywhere. I had to get to my children. This was a crazy dynamic; I was working at the seat of world power and feeling helpless and afraid because my community was on fire.

I remember the horrific traffic that was increasing on the roads with the worsening reports out of Baltimore. The closer to home I drove, the worse the traffic became. I was getting more agitated. The closer in mileage to home, the farther away I felt. These are my babies I had to pick up and make sure were safe. As a single parent, these are the two little people I work

35

hard and sacrifice for. I prayed that the Lord would keep them safe in this unfolding storm of hurt and anger. My mind was racing on many things. But I fought to get them into this world, and that fight to keep them alive and to thrive was not going to stop that day. My title of "mother" started with two difficult pregnancies at the ages of thirty-five and forty. In both pregnancies, each of my girls' heart rate dropped dangerously low and at times even stopped for my younger child. And for my older daughter, I almost lost my own life, as I had complications with double pneumonia immediately following my emergency induction of labor. From the moment I knew I was carrying them, I vowed to do my best for them, putting my needs on the back burner like so many parents have done, are doing, and will do. I wanted to keep my children from falling into any negativity that may have stunted them in any way.

As my journey home became longer and longer, another mother stepped up to help and was able to grab my girls from school and take them with her. They were safe! A wave of relief washed over me, calming anxieties stemming from the newness of this anger that had been building in the city for many, many years. But once I picked up my two girls, that's when we encountered the pickup truck boldly brandishing the Confederate flag that I described in Chapter 1. Yes, the driver and passengers of that truck have the First Amendment rights on their side, but that was not the time to throw gasoline on raw emotions and this fire that was smoldering.

Down that same road, 11.2 miles away and a thirty-three-minute drive, emotions were just as raw for parents, particularly Black mothers and fathers in Baltimore City who were searching for their kids at ground zero in the riots. I was not alone in efforts to find my children. Looking back on that day, I reflect on something Reverend Vanzant said during our phone interview for this book: "A mother's love is the presence of God that moves in human form regardless of whether you are partnered or unpartnered." She says it all stems from the growth of life in your being, and then you "mold and carve it in ways that impact the world." She takes the center of motherhood back to spirituality, saying, "I think that is a sacred work and that is why I believe it is such a powerful thing."

The mother of Trayvon Martin, Sybrina Fulton, contends she has "a different opinion than other people." When looking back at what happened that April 2015 day in Baltimore, Fulton says of the woman in the viral video, "She was trying to protect her child. She knew what was out there. She knew the streets were dangerous." Putting herself in those shoes, she feels, "Maybe I would have handled it that way. Maybe if I were in that situation." It is all about survival. "If you could save your son's life by whacking him a couple of times or punching him a couple of times, of course you are gonna do that."

For those who are judging, Fulton finds, "We can sit back now after the game, after everything is over and say I woulda have, shoulda have, but the fact remains that she was in a position where she coulda stopped him from going and getting arrested or even killed and she did!" At the end of the day, "We want our children to make it home safely!"

Judge Mablean Ephriam says there should be "more mothers like that," asserting that it is about "discipline!" She firmly offers, "Those laws in terms of how we discipline our children, and calling everything we do corporal punishment and parents being punished for disciplining their children, they need to cut that mess out! What that has done is tied the hands of the parents and leaves it up to the police." They are strong words, but the rationale is real from a mother to a child. "If you don't learn to fear me, your first point of authority, your mother or your father, you are not going to respect anyone else." Judge Ephriam finds our kids are caught in a cycle that stems from the lack of respect in the home. "That is why they are disrespecting police, because they don't have respect for authority."

Gwen Carr, the mother of Eric Garner, the Black man who died in a chokehold while in New York City police custody, said, "We used to live in the projects in downtown Brooklyn, and you always hear gunshots, and I would tell them . . . my younger son would always run to the back. I would say, 'Get out that window and get down on the floor, you don't know when one of those bullets are coming through the house.' I would make them lay down on the floor. We would start hearing gunfire. I would make them lay down on the floor. But they would sneak. Kids' curiosity, they would sneak to the window to see if anything happened, to see what was going on."

Gwen Carr knows a thing or two about motherhood. She also knows about hurt. Her husband died at the age of thirty-three, leaving her a young widow at twenty-seven with heartache, raising their kids ages five years old, four years old, and four months old. "That was my first real traumatic loss," remembers Carr. Then she lost her friend, who was also her sister-in-law, not long after her husband. Her sister-in-law died unexpectedly after a blood clot traveled to her lungs after the doctors reset her broken leg in the late 1970s. Four years later, more loss: her brother died of a blood disorder in 1982.

She worked through her hurt and kept moving forward and raised her kids along with her brother's kids. But death came knocking on her door again, and this time the blow was even closer. Her middle child, her second son, was killed in Troy, New York. He was robbed and killed while on vacation. She remembers, "We never actually found out who killed him." She was bedridden as a result of that death. The pain was more than she could bear, she said. "I went into a total depression. I just shut down. I lost about a hundred pounds after my first son's death. My family nursed me back to health."

Then in July 2015, Carr and her family were planning on a family reunion of sorts in Prospect Park in New York City, where the whole family would gather that Sunday. Everyone was looking forward to the event, including her oldest son, Eric. But earlier in the week, Carr says the police were called to break up a fight where Eric was involved, even though he had already stopped the brawl. Carr heard that her son was trying to broker peace on the street. But Eric was the only one left in front of the beauty store. All those involved in the fight left the scene. Mrs. Carr believes Eric was taken down by police because he was standing there, and police were familiar with him because he sold single cigarettes to raise money. Carr acknowledges the only reason it is illegal to sell a single cigarette is because "the government does not get its cut."

The chokehold was caught on several phones and cameras that also showed Eric gasping for air, saying, "I can't breathe!" Carr recalls the moment she learned of the police being involved in Eric's death, "When this happened to me, I thought that I would just take to my bed and just stay there. 'Cause when this happened to me, I thought that I just would wait for someone to wake me from this terrible nightmare."

Carr acknowledges that Eric's medical condition was real. She says his dream was to work with cars, but he couldn't because of his upper-respiratory condition. So she lost her first and second children "violently," and now her surviving child is her third one and her only daughter.

Jarrett also vividly remembers the viral video of a parent disciplining a child during the Baltimore riot, saying, "Maybe this shows you the difference of life experiences. I completely could tap into that fear. The only time I ever spanked my daughter was when she ran out in the street in front of a car. I was terrified! And I wanted to scare the living daylights out of her because I was so scared. And there are moms in this country that live in that fear, that I felt one time in my child's life every single day. I can't imagine living under that kind of fear, and yet that is what they are subjected to, and nonetheless they persevere and they get up and go to work and they work three jobs and they come home bone tired and they sit there and they try to get their children to focus on their homework."

Baltimorean Wes Moore said, of the young men participating in the riot, "We as Black men don't have the flexibility to say when the law determines when we become men. You don't become a Black man in this society at eighteen years old. You become a Black man much earlier. The idea of being a boy goes away much quicker particularly for our young Black men growing up in really difficult conditions."

Moore acknowledges police were there protecting structures and institutions in the city during that 2015 riot, but the disciplined teenager was going to get an awful coming-of-age lesson as his entrée into manhood for his association with the rebellious actions that ugly day. He was still a child but would be afforded the life lessons of a man. Moore says it was about Graham's "protective instinct" as a mother, as things may have been "clouded in his own mind." Moore understands the full thrust of a mother's love, using his mother as a prime example, and feels her motivation was not to take a "political stand" or to "prove a point." Moore says her motivation was to help him understand that the consequences are much higher with the long term than with what was in front of him, the anger of the day, and the heat of the moment that lasted several weeks in Baltimore.

As the woman in the viral video will be forever linked to the Baltimore riot, I was able to conduct a thirty-minute interview with her by phone, but she has since declined use of her quotes for this book. What I did take away from my conversation was that for this god-fearing woman, life is not easy as she remains vigilant to prevent an unbearable heartache, the loss of a child to the streets of Baltimore.

There are many mothers who must be pragmatic with issues surrounding family, financial stability, and survival. These issues are never more present than with the media accounts of Trayvon Martin and watching his parents after his death at the George Zimmerman trial, where Zimmerman was found not guilty of murder. The issue was compounded again with the Michael Brown death in Ferguson, Missouri, and it came into her backyard of Baltimore with the death of Freddie Gray, who died in Baltimore City Police custody, when it was found by the state's attorney's office that he should have never been arrested or even placed in police custody. Over and over again with every death of a Black male, parents' fears hit closer to home, and they hope it never touches the inside of their four walls.

Parents in economically challenged inner-city communities have a good understanding of all of the positives and the many examples of devastating negatives. Those negatives include many kids who do not feel the hope of a better day and succumb to what is offered in the streets and feel that is their destiny. It is a fact of their location, and it is hard for them to look beyond the boundaries of their ten-block radius. When I grew up, it was a common statement that people from Baltimore never venture out beyond their neighborhood. In many instances it was, and still is, true.

Saturday, April 23, 2016, at Morgan State University I moderated the African American Women's town hall event for the Hillary Clinton campaign in the few days before the Maryland primary election. That stage held three mothers who told their story about their dead children. One of those mothers was Gwen Carr. Carr said she talked with her son that morning, and they kept with their routine of telling each other "I love you" before they get off the phone. She said if she knew what she knows now, that morning of their last conversation, she would have kept him on the phone for hours.

Reverend Vanzant, a mother herself, affirms "a mother's love is the universal healer, I don't care who you are. What you do or where you come from. Lay your head on a mother's bosom and all gets right with the world, if she is a mother." People don't take that role as seriously as it is. You know the king is not the king simply because he inherits the throne. The king is the king because he was raised by a mother who understood his value, who understood his destiny, who understood his purpose. She had to make sure he was handled properly and fed properly. She had to make space in his life for him to be the royalty that he became. Every king has a mother. The better his relationship with his mother, the better king he is.

But what we have seen in part are some of the injustices of a system that were veiled, and now the covers are off with the accountability component being the visuals that are now being captured by cell phone cameras and beyond. The issue of criminal justice was front and center during the second term and fourth quarter of the Obama administration with the president calling for reform.

In this post-Obama era, a marker that erases the so-called postracial dynamic, the fact is that Blacks, particularly Black males, have to bear a heavy burden when it comes to confrontations with police in many communities across the country. Because of the accountability component of the videotaping of arrests, mothers now have some sliver of hope that the at-risk spiral for their Black children, particularly their sons, will get better. But that is just a small piece of a solution to a bigger problem in the criminal justice system. Eight years of President Barack Hussein Obama, a transformative president who came to Washington as a constitutional lawyer when he entered the US Senate, intentionally or unintentionally focused on this issue of young, at-risk minority males through the My Brother's Keeper program. For decades, this has been a pervasive issue in the Black community. When Barack Hussein Obama became President of the United States, he slowly evolved into a "rights president" with constitutional law as his backbone. He moved the pendulum on women's rights to include the Lilly Ledbetter Fair Pay Act. He moved the pendulum on the issue of same-sex marriage as he openly acknowledged that as president of all America, he must support the legal rights of all segments of the country. He was a president who boldly put the spotlight on policing and offered criminal justice reform to a system that has disproportionate negative numbers against Black and Brown persons who are negatively affected in the penal system in this country. On criminal justice reform, here is what the president said at the end of 2015 when I asked him what bill he did support, as there were concerns that none of the bills drastically cut into the system as hoped and intended by many in Washington:

All right. I've got April Ryan . . .

THE PRESIDENT: And, April, what I said was, is that I strongly support the Senate legislation that's already been put forward. I'm hopeful that the House can come up with legislation that follows the same principles, which is to make sure that we're doing sentencing reform, but we're also doing a better job in terms of reducing recidivism and providing support for ex-offenders. And if we can get those two bills together in a conference, then I'm somewhat optimistic that we're going to be able to make a difference.

Now, keep in mind, April, when you use the term "mass incarceration," statistically, the overwhelming majority of people who are incarcerated are in state prisons and state facilities for state crimes. We can only focus on federal law and federal crimes. And so there's still going to be a large population of individuals who are incarcerated even for nonviolent drug crimes, because this is a trend that started in the late '80s and '90s and accelerated at the state levels.

But if we can show at the federal level that we can be smart on crime, more cost-effective, more just, more proportionate, then we can set a trend for other states to follow, as well. And that's our hope. This is not going to be something that's reversed overnight.

So just to go back to my general principle, April, it took twenty years for us to get to the point we are now. And it will be twenty years, probably, before we reverse some of these major trends.

Okay, everybody, I got to get to *Star Wars*. Thank you. Thank you, guys. Appreciate you. Merry Christmas, everybody.

Now, the average mother who is wringing her hands over her child's welfare looks to hope in the long term, not the short term. Eventually, there could be equity in a system that is proven not to be fair to all. This is a real part of life for many families who have "a broken hood," from parenthood to neighborhood. But nonetheless, issues of real life slap mothers the hardest even as they have to address the issues in their brokenness. When you deal with minority America and the truth of the 'hood, no matter what level of dysfunction, the pain is real and about survival for many moms who have played mother and father and even grandparent to sons and daughters in need of that extra measure of support to get them to the next level. It is not a misstatement for me to say that we as a nation are still wrapped up in emotion and trying to figure what happened in Ferguson, Missouri.

As we look over the years, mothers have had to "conspire" to keep their children safe, according to Baltimore native Bishop Vashti McKenzie of African Methodist Episcopal (AME). It is a histories-old issue, as McKenzie says, "Black mothers have been losing their children since they have been in America." She reviews history, acknowledging that since our inception in this country Black women were "objectified" in the beginning as "jezeb-els," "raped," they were "bred to produce children every year" for fifteen to twenty years. All the while they were in the fields or doing whatever service they were charged to do. McKenzie says, "Black women from the beginning were threatened if they did not do the sexual favors. Then their children were sold off. Mothers had to watch their children sold off." There were other just as egregious matters. If they were girl children, mothers had to bring their girl children to the masters to introduce them to sex. McKenzie asks, "Can you imagine that, saying, 'Okay baby now, I am going to take you to this room and just whatever they do, come home and we will cry about it together.'"

The course of history shows the path for Black mothers was different with McKenzie's statement, "There is always something you had to do dif-ferent from any other population because they were sold off, objectified, murdered or killed or maimed." Men and women told their stories. "This is not conjecture. This is not a myth; it is not a legend." Bishop McKenzie compares yesterday to what is currently happening. She contends, "Now you take a look at Black mothers doing what they can to raise their children before they let them go. It all points back to the universal love of the story of Moses. It is about conspiring to keep children alive." McKenzie adds, "That is what happened to the Hebrews when they were in Goshen. They had to conspire to keep the boys alive. The girls were allowed to live. What did they do in slavery time? They had to conspire to keep the children alive. What are we doing now? We are conspiring to keep our children alive. We are trying to teach them and share with them things that other parents don't have to share with their children that this is how you are going to stay alive, that this is how you are going to get home safely today. To conspire against the evil of this world, against whatever the proclivities of the fears and pho-bias that other people have that a ten-year-old Black child is a threat, that a sixteen-year-old girl in a bikini in McKinney, Texas, somehow is threaten-ing a two-hundred-pound police officer with a gun on his hip. But he has to throw her down to the ground and put his knee in her back to keep her down to the ground. That a twelve-year-old Tamir Rice with a toy gun in his hand. . . . The color of your skin determines if the police talk to you, if we give you a chance."

Bishop McKenzie's statements are supported by the *Washington Post* ar-ticle "990 People Shot Dead by Police in 2015." The graphs and data findings during the 12 months of that year indicated that of the 990 police-involved fatal shootings, Blacks were 2.5 times more likely to be killed by officers than Whites.

McKenzie's argument is valid. She also uses the analogy of a kindergarten kid jostling a White kid in school, and the Black kid is suspended and handcuffed and in the back of a police car at five or six years old. She acknowledges this is now going into other communities, but when it happens to them there is a double standard. They are sick and need help compared to the harsh punishment for our kids. If you think that is far-fetched, it is not. The expulsion rates for minority preschoolers are higher than for Whites. The *Civil Rights Data Collection Snapshot: School Discipline Issue Brief No. 1 March 2014* finds:

> Black children represent 18% of preschool enrollment, but 48% of preschool children receiving more than one out-of-school suspension; in comparison, white students represent 43% of preschool enrollment but 26% of preschool children receiving more than one out-of-school suspension. Boys represent 79% of preschool children suspended once and 82% of preschool children suspended multiple times, although boys represent 54% of preschool enrollment.

So many Black mothers had to "conspire" and "network and work together" and strategize for their children's future. McKenzie says it has always been that way since we have been in America.

And this issue goes so much deeper than what we often see today played over and over again on the news and on the thirty-second YouTube clips. Senator Cory Booker says, "It is ridiculous to me that there is not a network raising our kids anymore." He feels this story is not unique in how a mother is alone in her battle to keep her child from succumbing to the meanness and ugliness of the streets. Booker says, "I know right now that we would drastically reduce juvenile violence all across our country, juvenile crime, if we just had mentoring. If people like me and others mentor, if people in our community said, 'Hey, I am going to do four hours a month,' the data is clear. Four hours a month of an adult being in a child's life dramatically lowers their involvement in crime. Dramatically lowers their unsafe sex practices and dramatically elevates their success in school. But yet we have waiting lists all around the country of mothers looking for mentors for their kids."

Mentorship is yet another form of parenting and creates the very real dynamic that motherhood is not always biological. There was a time when the African proverb of "it takes a village to raise a child" held true. More than fifty years ago there were mothers that participated in the movement, the civil rights struggle. For Congressman John Lewis the mothers of the civil rights movement were also his example. Their dream was for a better day.

Lewis recalls more than a half century ago, "If it hadn't been for these unbelievable women, I don't know what would have happened to the movement. It was all over the South. And one day before I leave this world planet, leave this world, most of them are probably gone on [passed away], but I would love to go back to some of the places, and I do from time to time. They were just ordinary women, brave and courageous, and many of them you didn't know their names." With emotion, the iconic civil rights leader says, "But they were there! In the mass meetings, the rallies, when there was a march, they were there! It was countless numbers of mothers. Some of the people had very little of anything. But they were so committed, so dedicated."

He recalls, "There were mothers living in housing projects in Selma; in Americus, Georgia; Albany, Georgia; in Birmingham. They shared with us the little they had. Then part of the time in Selma, I stayed with a family in a housing project 'cause we didn't have a freedom house all the time, or money to stay in some hotel. A lot of the places, not until '64, they weren't even desegregated. So you go to southwest Georgia, go to the Delta Mississippi, people took us in. We stayed in the homes with families and it was risky. I mean really dangerous. In Mississippi they referred to all of us as those 'Freedom Riders.' They literally took us in."

During that time the families had very little. Lewis and other civil rights activists could sleep in a bed or on a pallet of three or four quilts on the floor to prevent the feel of the hardness of the floor. "I saw that over and over and over again." They would also eat food from the gardens of those who had them. They would eat beans and peas. Lewis says, "It was not the best food, but you were full. They would make Kool-Aid and lemonade."

There are so many stories about fighting to get out of that cumbersome statistical factoring. The fight is real! Sybrina Fulton, the mother of Trayvon Martin, says, "What is happening now, this country is in a crisis. . . . Why is it open season on African American men? I want this season to be over!"

Fulton sternly says, "It just seems that African Americans are treated so much differently from anybody else. . . . People need to be made aware of it and recognize that that is what is going on and stop pretending it is not happening!" It is more than personal for her, "Our children are being murdered. Our children are being killed. Our children are not being allowed to grow up for some of the same things that their kids are doing!"

Fulton says of her son's murder and other Blacks being killed, "At the end of the day, when you don't get justice it just seems so unfair. Like nobody is paying attention to what is going on. Nobody is caring about what is going on in that particular race." Fulton likens it to "what I call the ostrich effect, when you stick your head in the sand and pretend like you don't know it is happening. But it is still going on around you!" She is clearly calling on the government to take a more active role.

Reflecting on all that has been said, my first recollections of the public conversations about these parent-to-child talks were from the great Harlem Renaissance writer and poet Langston Hughes with "Mother to Son." My mother would recite this first line, one of the most famous lines in Black literary culture: "Well, son, I'll tell you: Life for me ain't been no crystal stair."

I delved deeper into the poem. It is about a mother's conversation with her son generally about race in this country and how hard it is for her, but she has the fortitude to continue to climb no matter the struggle. I see beauty in the struggle, in every step of that struggle, particularly for those women and mothers who fight against the racist and societal odds. There is an outpouring of love for their children because they want to give them the opportunities they did not have and in many cases could not afford. Yes, and Langston Hughes says there have been tacks and splinters in the stairs, but she is still climbing. That mother offered truths about the harsh realities, not sugarcoating it for her child to navigate this life with a mother's love.

· 4 ·

The N-Word

$\mathcal{A}$ mother's love and her language are crucial in the shaping of societal concepts, perceptions, and reactions according to Dr. Milo Dodson, in his essay "A Mother's Love and a Mother's Language."

Language is inherently a multicultural exchange. Individuals from various backgrounds interact using combinations of words that will not just shape their understanding of each other, but can impact and change their view of the world.

Why? Because words are powerful. The ineptitudes and decline of positive interpersonal relationships start as early as childhood, through bullying, largely due to the language being used. Sticks and stones may break your bones, but use of the n-word has been linked to racism and institutional violence.

Similar to linguist Geneva Smitherman, I believe race is a defining feature of African American language. Language is a powerful force in human interactions and is a major component of individuals' conceptualizations of their personal lexicon. Language is not just created by our intentions, but also by how people hear and experience what we say. The contexts in which we use language are essential to how both speakers and listeners create meaning.

Among many things parents teach their children is the use and function of language. Fundamental to the discussion of the n-word is an understanding of the original historical use of the word *nigger*. The word *nigger* has been intended to disparage Black persons living in America since its inception. Slave owners used it against their slaves to dehumanize them and to assert racial superiority. Although the word *nigger* is a volatile and contentious racial epithet, variations on the word have emerged to "represent" different, nonoffensive meanings. For example, some individuals use the spelling *nigga* and argue that this version of the word allows for a reshaping

47

of the word *nigger* into an empowering one or a term of endearment. Conversely, other individuals argue that using *nigga* only further perpetuates negative stereotypes of African Americans and that despite good intentions, the word should not be used.

In my dissertation, I investigated five linguistic ideologies: (1) Indexicality (i.e., the word *nigga* can have different meanings depending on the social situation or cultural context); (2) Personalism (i.e., the deciding factor in determining the meaning for the word *nigga* comes from the beliefs and/or intentions of the speaker); (3) Reshaping (i.e., the word *nigga* is a reshaping of the historical racial slur nigger); (4) Baptismal (i.e., the word *nigga* can never be harmless because of its original meaning as a racial slur); and (5) Performative (i.e., the word *nigga* should not be used, since it may be emotionally harmful to those who hear it).

Findings from hierarchical multiple regressions indicated linguistic ideologies accounted for a significant amount of variance in levels of acceptance for use of the word *nigga* in each of three contexts: (1) used among Black individuals; (2) used among non-Black individuals; and (3) used in public spaces. Reshaping ideology (i.e., the word *nigga* is a reshaping of the historical racial slur *nigger*) was a unique predictor of each of these contexts; greater endorsement of a Reshaping ideology was related to greater levels of acceptance of the use of the word *nigga* across each of the three contexts.

Whether or not mothers use the word, discussing the n-word indubitably presents a crucial opportunity to teach children about their heritage, race, and the assumptions others make about race. There is not just one way to be Black.

My humble words to all the mothers: Educate children about the importance of using empowering language so they open their minds to a world of self-expression in which you share unconditional love with them every step of the way.

Dr. Dodson's words bring me back to one of the ugly truths of our past. In March 2015 the first Black U.S. president, Barack Hussein Obama, traveled to Alabama on Air Force One to mark the fiftieth anniversary of the Bloody Sunday march in Selma. Many decades prior to this visit there had been work toward a shift in racial attitudes but some of our fellow White Americans did not like the changes, and subsequently Blacks were called *nigger* openly without an apology. Alabama was the setting for the events of more than fifty years prior. Brutal does not begin to describe the atrocities. Accompanying the ugliness of that past was the word *nigger*, the hurtful adjective, noun, verb, and adverb used in almost every newscast, by local and national leaders opposed to the move for equality. They described the Black Americans just wanting the right to vote and any other right that would place Blacks on equal footing with Whites with that ugly word. A few months later in June 2015, President Obama was interviewed by an alternative pop culture broadcaster in his garage. The reason that interviewer was selected was because of his popularity and his counterculture familiarity with reaching a vast number of people.

The president used the interviewer's unorthodox means to throw a dart that hit its intended bull's-eye. President Obama used the n-word during the videotaped conversation about racism. It was used in a sentence to symbolize that "we" collectively as a people are still hung up on matters of race in this nation. The chatter about the president's comments went viral. He proved we are still hypersensitive over anything about race. That was a major week in America. The president made that comment, the Confederate flag was taken down from public buildings in South Carolina, and President Obama became preacher in chief at the end of that week when he delivered a eulogy for the reverend who had been shot down with eight others at Mother Emanuel Church in Charleston, South Carolina. He ended his spiritually rousing talk with his solo singing of the Negro spiritual "Amazing Grace." That song punctuated the moment, as it was written by a White man whose spirit was in turmoil over the inhumanity of slavery, in which people were stolen from their homes, overcrowded on wooden shelves in the bottom of ships, and taken on a long, six-month-or-more journey to America to be sold into the forced bondage of terrorized free labor.

As for his intentional and teachable-moment use of the word *nigger*, Valerie Jarrett said, "He [President Obama] is not afraid of a word." She went on to say, "For the point he was trying to make that was the right word."

But her statement begs the question about the general use of the word. She says, "It depends how you use it. It can be used in a very destructive, hateful way. That is not how he used it. He used it in context and it was totally appropriate. We shouldn't be afraid of a word. We shouldn't abuse a word. A word is a tool. So the answer depends on how you intend to use that tool. Unfortunately, the word has been used as a very destructive, hateful tool." Jarrett did not know what was coming months later at the Washington Hilton at the White House Correspondents' Association (WHCA) dinner.

At that dinner, the last dinner for President Obama, the shock and awe of the n-word was on full display for a mixed crowd of mostly White attendees. Presidents, as in the past, are the guests of honor and are roasted. That is fair game. Well, it is expected game for that night. But the April 30, 2016, dinner gave attendees an uncomfortable package to handle. According to the transcript from the *Washington Post*'s May 1 article, "Larry Wilmore's Harshest Burns in His White House Correspondents' Dinner Speech," Wilmore ended the night telling the president how much he loved him and what he achieved as a Black man, but then ended it with the worst word in the American language. According to the transcript, Wilmore used the "a," not the "er," ending. Either way, it is just as bad, as the "a" is derived from the "er." According to columnist Jonathan Capehart and his *Washington Post* opinion column titled "Why Larry Wilmore Is Not "My N- - - - -," the transcript of Wilmore's words that night was "When I was a kid, I lived in a country where people couldn't accept a Black quarterback. Now think about that. A Black man was thought by his mere color not good enough to lead a football team—and now, to live in your time, Mr. President, when a Black man can lead the entire free world. Words alone do me no justice. So, Mr. President, if I'm going to keep it 100: Yo, Barry, you did it, my *nigger*. You did it."

The Black people I came across that night were more than upset. They were furious about the level of disrespect. The people I talked with included the head of the NAACP, the former head of the Republican Party, TV show hosts, comedians, people in the Obama administration, and a host of others. Most of them were so angry.

Wilmore's heartfelt words were quickly forgotten with his choice of ugly words. He was rehearsed as to what he was going to do, I was told by a credible, highly regarded network personality who talked to Wilmore after his skit. He told that person he and his team went back and forth about the use of the word. Apparently he decided to use the provocative, ill-fitting word no matter whom it hurt.

This was not a teachable moment but a time for a thirsty comedian to cross the boundaries of courtesy, respect, and etiquette. In his comedic skit that immediately followed President Obama, Wilmore, in the short time at the podium before a crowd of well over 2,500 seated guests and scores of people watching on international television, broke the code. In his skit, he teed up for what would leave many Black people and others in the politically charged and celebrity- and journalist-filled room stunned and speechless after he found ways to use the words *negro nation*, *thugs*, and *jigaboo* and ended the night with telling President Obama, "You are my" either "*nigga*" or "*nigger*." Either is unacceptable. So he started out rocky. According to the *Washington Post*, Wilmore said, "Welcome to Negro Night here in Washington. Or as Fox News will report, 'Two thugs disrupt elegant dinner in DC.'" According to the *Daily Beast* and the article "'Larry Wilmore Roasts the Press in White House Correspondents' Monologue" by Matt Willstein on April 20, 2016, Wilmore's take on Ben Carson was that he was appraising 'tremendous president' Andrew Jackson. The Treasury Department had recently announced it was considering replacing Jackson on the 20 dollar bill with Tubman. "From the grave, Andrew Jackson said, 'What did that *jigaboo* say?'" he joked.

There was a very uncomfortable gasp in the room followed by silence when he finished it all. Folks were left in disbelief about the words he used to describe the first Black president, number forty-four. Those words were also the last words of a dinner that will go down in the history books. That lingering negativity will be perpetually available on the Internet, looping around forever, referencing the first Black president for his last dinner with the White House Press Corps, a group that he worked with for eight years. To Larry Wilmore I say thank you for marring history. The evening lost its luster because he took us back down a very painful road in front of a mixed audience and then made everyone in that room uncomfortable. It was ugly and unnecessary.

Whoopi Goldberg left the room immediately with facial expressions during the night that told of her upset with the comedian. Armstrong Williams said he was embarrassed. Michael Steele said it was a shame those were the last words for the first Black president at his last WHCA dinner. I ran into the head of the NAACP, Cornell Brooks, who talked to many participants that evening who were in disbelief. Joy Behar said his entire act bombed and she was offended by the words. He is one of the few Black people to perform at the dinner in its 102-year history. I am only one of three Black people in the history of the WHCA to ever hold a seat on that prestigious all-White board. That group, more than seventy years ago, told a Black reporter by the name of Harry McAlpin that if he stepped on White reporters' toes during a press conference there would be a riot. We have been striving to move the ball forward and now this! Wilmore's poor word choice was the topic of conversation everywhere that weekend after he delivered his cutting statements.

A reporter who was the target of some of the tasteless jokes said the Obamas laughed when Wilmore used the word *jigaboo*. I said they had to laugh to keep from crying; that is, if they had reacted it would have been a news item. There was an eerie and awkward silence in the room once he put those words in the atmosphere. Normally people are talking, laughing, and remembering with joy what just was said. Instead, people were brought back to painful memories or had to think of a disturbing past. I talked to CBS White House correspondent Bill Plante, who covered Bloody Sunday over fifty years ago. He affirmed that the words uttered by Wilmore at the dinner had been used decades ago with hate and anger during that historic march. Did Wilmore really understand what he had done? Did he know the history of the dinner, the history of Black people and that word, and what it means to respect the office of the presidency?

Interestingly enough, in 2009, Wanda Sykes revealed that the WHCA told her not to use the n-word or the f-bomb. She discussed the issue in the May 11, 2009, article "Obama Administration Distances Itself from Wanda Sykes; 9/11; Rush Limbaugh Joke" by David Saltonstall for the *Daily News*. In the article's last paragraph, it shows she had enough discernment to understand you do not say certain things to the president of the United States. The reporter wrote, "Sykes took offense that she was warned 'not to say the f-word or the n-word' before her bit."

"They really think I was going to say that to the President?" she told *Extra*.

Well, Wilmore did not think enough of himself or the president not to use that word. The onslaught began as the word rolled off his tongue and he pounded his chest as if the words were from the heart. When in doubt, leave it out. Well, he did not, and the rest is painful history that we can read and watch over and over again for the last White House Correspondents' Association dinner of the first Black president. That was simply wrong in my opinion.

It definitely was a slap in the face and a punch to the gut. For many of the African Americans in that room it felt like he may have well called each and every one of us that word. How ugly! How base! What angers me more about this is he and his crew debated about using it. He knew it was wrong. He knew it would get attention. It was too much!

White House Correspondents' Association member and dinner historian George Condon says there are no examples of racial or racist words used at any time during post–World War II dinners. But when it comes to pre–World War II dinners, Condon says, "Amos and Andy were the emcees at the 1930 dinner. They weren't in blackface," and he says they didn't do their routine in dialect during those times, as racial humor was very possible. Between 1946 and 2016, entertainers have included Duke Ellington, Nat King Cole, Dizzy Gillespie, Aretha Franklin, Godfrey Cambridge, Mahalia Jackson, Count Basie, Sinbad, Ray Charles, Cedric the Entertainer, Wanda Sykes, Oscar "Papa" Celestin, the tap-dancing Step Brothers, drummer Samuel Baby Lovett, and blues singer Julia Lee.

Larry Wilmore used *nigga*, a derivative of the word *nigger*. It was not just inappropriate, it was offensive. My mother always taught me it is not what they call you but what you answer to. Well, that night I did not answer to it, but I felt like it was me and every Black in that room that he called a *nigger*. It was simply a lack of class, dignity, and respect.

The Monday after the dinner, May 2, 2016, the White House press secretary Josh Earnest was peppered with questions in the briefing room on various topics to include the president's impending trip to Flint, Michigan, where he would see firsthand what was happening with the drinking water crisis. But there was one subject that was looming, the words of Larry Wilmore. Over the weekend, I asked Josh Earnest what the president was thinking following the previous night's illustrious dinner. He said he had not talked with the president since the event. I advised Earnest to be prepared for the question on Monday. So of course I asked the question. To his credit, he came with an answer after talking with the president about it. We danced around verbally in the briefing room, particularly focusing on the n-word. Here is the transcript of that question and answer session.

Q: Josh, I want to follow up kind of on Justin. And I have another question. It's kind of an urban week for the President. He's traveling to Flint and then he's also doing the Howard University commencement. Are there any threads that are going to travel through to both of his speeches, in Flint and in Howard? And will he be making any news when it comes to the urban front?

MR. EARNEST: Well, stay tuned. I'm not in a position to begin previewing the President's commencement address at Howard at this point, but the President and his team have been working on his speech for a couple of weeks now. But check in later this week, and maybe I'll be able to give you a better sense of what the President's plans are for that speech.

Q: All right. And I also want to ask you—this weekend at his last White House Correspondents' Association Dinner, he gave jokes, got some ribbing. What did he think about the final words that were delivered to him and of him, the President of the United States—a word that is one of the worst words many people say you could say to anyone, that's gone down in history? What did he think about that? What's his reaction?

MR. EARNEST: Well, April, I think the first thing that I would observe is that any comedian who signed up to follow President Obama at the White House Correspondents' Dinner is assuming one of the most difficult tasks in comedy. Just by nature of the engagement, that's a tough job, following the President of the United States.

President Obama also, over the years, has shown himself to be rather adept at delivering a speech that consists primarily of one- or two-liners, and the President enjoys that opportunity.

So the point is that Mr. Wilmore had a difficult job that he was facing on Saturday, and the President's expectation is he took—as Mr. Wilmore took on that responsibility, is that comedians are going to go right up to the line.

Q: Did he cross the line? Many African Americans in that room, to include Civil Rights leaders, Black comedians, were very appalled. Even members of the Republican Party—Black Republicans were upset, Black Democrats were upset. People felt that not just throwing it at him, but throwing it at them, and also it diminished the office of the presidency and it diminished him. Did he cross the line?

MR. EARNEST: April, what I would say is that it's not the first time that people, on the Monday after the White House Correspondents' Dinner, that some people have observed that the comedian on Saturday night crossed the line. That happened in 2006, after Stephen Colbert delivered his speech. There were many people who felt like he had overstepped his bounds in delivering his remarks. To a lesser extent, many people made the same observation about the presentation of Wanda Sykes in 2009. So it's not the first time that we've had a conversation like this in which these kinds of concerns have been raised or expressed.

Look, I had an opportunity to speak to the President about this briefly this morning, and he said that he appreciated the spirit of the sentiments that Mr. Wilmore expressed. He ended his speech by saying that he couldn't put into words the pride that he felt in the President. And he made the observation that our country has made remarkable progress just in his lifetime—from not being willing to accept an African American quarterback, to electing and reelecting an African American not just to lead the United States, but to lead the free world. Again, I take Mr. Wilmore at his words that he found that to be a powerful transformation just in his lifetime, and something that he seemed to be pretty obviously proud of.

Q: Did Mr. Wilmore's use of freedom of speech give the President's detractors fodder now to be able to call him that and call others that?

MR. EARNEST: Well, I have no idea what impact Larry Wilmore's speech is going to have on the President's critics, and I don't think I'm going to spend much time worrying about it.

Q: I understand that there is a conversation about that word. The President, in June of last year, used it as a teaching moment to show that issues of race are still a problem in this country. But Wilmore used it for the President somewhat as a butt of the joke. And you were in that room, as well as I was. There was an eerie, awkward silence and quietness. And people didn't know how to handle that.

MR. EARNEST: Well, April, I know this is a word that does—let me say it this way: I'm confident that Mr. Wilmore used the word by design. He was seeking to be provocative. But I think any reading of his comments makes clear he was not using the President as the butt of a joke. So what is true is that this is a tough assignment that any comedian takes on when they sign up for this job. And the President's expectation when he walks in that room is that that comedian and other people are going to get much closer to the line than they ordinarily would as they try to make a joke.

Q: I just want to be very clear: So the President is okay with his use and how he used the n-word, "jigaboo," "Negro night," and "thug"?

MR. EARNEST: Well, April, I'll just restate what I said before, which is that the President expressed—well, what the President said is that he appreciated the spirit of Mr. Wilmore's expressions on Saturday night.

What is interesting about the span of that week, around the president's last dinner, is there was another issue surrounding the n-word, this time with Malia Obama and her choice of Harvard as the college she would attend. A news blog took down some of the comments from those who responded to the article. The n-word was used often on that blog in reference to her and the college choice she made as well as what was perceived as a privilege for her to attend an Ivy League school.

Via e-mail, I asked actor, writer, and director Erika Alexander (from the TV show *Livin' Single* among many others) her thoughts on the word and its usage. She has strong feelings on the daily use of the word by the Black community:

> I don't think about the word NIGGER very often. See, I was raised in Flagstaff, AZ and in my first years I had a German-Lutheran upbringing that saved me from having that word, nigger, drilled into my mind's eye or my working vocabulary. And to this day it rarely comes up . . . except when I'm around other Black people.
>
> I find that curious and, frankly, depressing. That I must go to Black neighborhoods to hear the word nigger. I hear it in our music, blasting from a passing radio or inside hair salons replaying the nigger song of the day, competing for dominance from the dryers' howl. It is most often served up as a side dish of sloppy talk from Black people. We even brag about it. It's authentic. Keeping it real. Its power is mythological. My people, WE pass it around, person to person, like a do-it-or-else chain-letter virus. I think that speaks to a successful branding campaign from the White racist who invented it, right? I mean, when the ugly brand you create is fully adopted and glorified by its target audience . . . you've got synergy. LOL. You've won . . . Not LOL.

Rae Dawn Chong, a writer, director, and actor known for countless films like *Quest for Fire*, *Commando*, and *The Color Purple*, says this by e-mail about the n-word:

> Let me be VERY clear. I have been in hot water using it in a historical way (Oprah thing), but I think it is a word that has both positive uses and negative and it saddens me that we have so many keepers of the gate regarding the word. Kendrick Lamar can use it because he lives in Compton and is Ghetto royalty. Gawd forbid someone who isn't all that uses the word correctly and every stripe of fool calls us out for being racist, which ironically is racist. It irritates me . . . but then again we are a wounded population with at least 1000 years of recovery ahead of us. So I get why we—most of

us—cannot bandy the word around without causing massive trouble. The word is charged for a reason, but funny enough I think avoiding it gives it way too much negative charge. I say take it back, use it, but change the charge. Disarm it.

Judge Mablean Ephriam, of the TV show *Justice with Judge Mablean,* said that her late mother (Mable) was born in Mississippi in 1911 in a segregated South. She told her children of those experiences. The family moved from Mississippi in 1955 to Los Angeles, where Judge Ephriam says her mother taught her children about the Black race and the White race. Her mom told her of the "distinction between the races and the segregated America and what they believed, that Whites were better and Blacks were inferior." Mother Mabel gave her opinion on the matter, saying to her young children, "They are no better than you. They think they are, but they are no better than you. We are all God's children and God made all of us and we are equal." She made those statements as the stark reality was that the kids knew the laws upheld the segregated facilities and only allowed Whites in certain places and Blacks in other places, not allowing the sides to meet or coexist.

Remembering those life lessons her mother taught, Judge Ephriam's mom also tempered that with the message that "you have to love everybody." She held that and practiced those words until the 1960s, when she saw the visuals of the civil rights movement right in front of her eyes on TV with Rosa Parks, the death of the four little girls, attack dogs, the use of water hoses, and on and on.

Her first personal, real contact with racism was when she began her college education at Pitzer, an all-White college in Claremont, California. Her education, up until high school was at all-Black facilities. At her "first parents' weekend" she met her roommate's disgruntled, vocal, and racially insensitive father. The roommate's father asked who was his daughter's roommate, and when he found out his daughter's roommate was Black, he said, "She is living with a *nigger*? I have got to take my baby out of that room with that *nigger*." The father threatened to take his money out of the private school if the girls were not separated. This behavior was in complete contrast to what her mother taught her about equality and positive self-esteem.

★ ★ ★

For me, as I look at the common overuse of "the word," that word strikes a mighty verbal blow and is still used too frequently today. There is not a dearth of use for this offensive word that for some remains an albatross around the Black community's neck. If we are completely honest with ourselves, many of us, Black and White, and people of all backgrounds have allowed that word to roll off the tongue. For others, the word lies dormant in many minds because of the harshness it elicits from memories of a painful and deadly past. Polite company cringes at the use of the word; others have no problem with its use. Our singers, comedians, and folks in the entertainment industry give us the audio and the visuals with its use, in abundance. Some have tried to say its constant use is cathartic because they are taking the sting out of the negative by turning it into a positive. But what remains for some after the initial attention grab is the reminder of the weight and ugliness from the past.

I clearly remember growing up in the Baltimore area being told by my mother that the word was offensive and wrong. My dad was a different story. He used the word a lot. He was one of those Black people where it was emblazoned into their vocabulary, particularly when they were upset. He was not alone; other family members, particularly from the older set, both male and female, used the word in jest and when it is time to use strong language, as if to cut you. You have to remember that word was in the face of Black people all the time, and it is no wonder there are many older Blacks who easily still use it. I kept wondering why the word was used so commonly yet considered so bad. Whenever I did not know or understand the meaning of a word, my mother wanted me to expand my mind, and I did just as she commonly requested. In the 1970s in our Northeast Baltimore home, I grabbed our family dictionary, an old blue linen hardbound book with yellowing pages. It was indeed well worn from use. At the time, when I looked for the word, I remember seeing part of the definition to include the word *slow* without a reference to race or color. But today, using many online dictionaries and the one embedded in my computer, the definitions have expanded to include the racial dynamic. In 2015 the definitions are consistently reminding the reader that it is one of the most negative words of all time. The current definitions of the word in most of the dictionary sources contend it is the most offensive word of the day with French and Spanish origin, from the late seventeenth century, describing the word *black*.

During the 1950s and 1960s the push was for equality and first-class citizenship. The word was commonly used, particularly by White people in their everyday conversations, to refer to Blacks. And it was used by Blacks who had lost self-identity and let ignorance define them. Unfortunately for many of us, we answered the call by now using the very words they used to call us. Progress has been made concerning the treatment of Black people with the Civil Rights Act and then the Voting Rights Act. In the late 1960s with all the strides made to stop segregation in public places, that one ugly, nasty word still remains. In the 1960s and 1970s, with the revival of Richard Pryor's career, the word *nigger* was prominent. His shock-and-awe use of the word propelled him to iconic status because no other high-profile entertainer with the massive reach he garnered was using it like he did as a Black man, almost making it palatable again. Pryor, a man who had a hard life growing up, used the word everywhere, in front of mixed crowds, on TV, and on his award-winning albums. *That Nigger's Crazy* went gold and *Bicentennial Nigger* won a Grammy.

I am by no means blaming Richard Pryor for not letting the word die, but instead I am pointing out how, throughout history the word continues to find a prominent home for its controversial display. What is more incredible is that Pryor had an epiphany when it came to using the word. His atonement was real and so was his reuse of the word. Yet Harry Belafonte marvels at the body of Pryor's work and does not believe "using the n-word set us back." During a phone interview, Belafonte said, "I think what it did was reach into the deepest recesses of our struggle of our pain, and put a word on the table for use and debate that took it out of the closet and here is what this word has done to the American fabric. Those of us of color who use the word have one set of references and applications and those not of African descent who use the word, usually use the word to crucify and contain and to see the object of that word as egregious, of lesser substance, of lesser value, of lesser quality than others."

Belafonte went on to say, "What has since happened is that the word no longer has the immediate application that it did back in the 1950s and 1960s when it began to become so pervasive as used by people as gifted as Richard Pryor was."

Loni Love, *The Real* talk show host, actress, and stand-up comedian, says, "For me personally, I don't, in my stand-up routine, I don't use the word, neither one of them." She says neither the "er" or "a" is used. "I don't allow people who open for me to use it either because I find my audiences to be very mainstream and I don't want to use that type of slang in front of them." Certainly her stand-up is colorful in many ways and can be blue at some points in her sketches, but the n-word is not allowed. She says growing up in the projects of Detroit, she did not hear the word nor was she called the word until she attended college in Texas. Love remembers, "Of course it was some White people that called me that. And that is when I realized that was the term that was slang for Black people. Until then in my whole growing up, I never had to deal with it, and I am from Detroit and the projects."

New Jersey Senator Cory Booker recalls that as a kid he heard those Pryor jokes. "From my time as a kid I listened to Richard Pryor records with my father. I am sure I laughed with jokes and things like that." But when it comes to the use of the n-word, Booker believes in the First Amendment, freedom of speech. His thought, "I believe people have the right to express themselves however they want and that's something I will defend. It is a part of our Constitution. I don't want to dictate what other people should say." However, the senator says his own personal belief is that "we are all agents of love here. . . . I think our mission in this world is to spread goodness, kindness, love, decency, and mercy." Booker's belief is, "We should watch our language." He contends his faith says, "There is power in the word. What you speak literally can manifest reality. Why would I choose to say things in any way that would be demeaning to others? Why would I give life to something as I speak it into the world that could be used to undermine someone's self-esteem, self-concept, that could give somebody else permission to say things that are demeaning? So I choose not to use that word in any routine way. I just think, if I want to live a life committed to elevation, I want to use words to elevate. If I want and am committed to a life of love, I want to use words that are loving. And I am just hopeful."

But it is clear he does not want the word in his mouth. "I can't force anybody on what to say. I am not the thought police or the word police, but I know the most powerful impact in this world is what I do, not what I say. I want to live a life that is the best possible in accordance with my values and live the best version of me possible. What that means is not only how I conduct myself but what comes out of my mouth. I definitely had things come out of my mouth that I regretted, had things come out of my mouth that reflected the lesser of me. But I am going to strive always to be the best version of myself and that means, for me, not using those words."

Reverend Iyanla Vanzant, author and spiritual coach, has similar thoughts to those of Senator Booker, saying, "As a spiritual technician, I believe in the power of words. People today will soon say the 23rd Psalm when they are in trouble because of the power of the word. That word *nigger* has a power, and it is a disempowering energy."

She looks at her own personal experience as a mother: "I told my son, when my son used it or when my son did things, that is inappropriate for you." No matter the use of *nigga* or *nigger*, Vanzant says it is wrong, and people who say they have changed the meaning "can justify anything. All things are permissible, but not everything is productive. All things can be done, but not everything has a positive influence."

Wes Moore, author and Baltimore native, also is vehemently against the use of the n-word, saying, "I do not use it. I don't let anyone use it talking about me or talking to me. I don't like it. When I hear people say we will take the power of the meaning from the derogatory terms that other people have come up about them, and somehow because we say it now then it becomes useful or it becomes power or a point of power—there are other words that can be used to describe my power without having to take up someone else's words and think that somehow I can reinvent it. . . . I don't understand the sense of potency that word somehow has in certain people's minds because somehow you drop the 'er' and turn it into an 'a.'"

Vanzant, like Moore, contends, "I will never call another person of color a *nigger*. I will never call another woman a bitch . . . ever, ever, unless I am explaining it." Vanzant carefully, with a smile in her voice, examines the construct of the word *bitch*, using its acronym to define it as "a Broad In Total Control of Herself!" But in reality, the dictionary defines the word as a female dog, wolf, fox, or otter. The dictionary also deemed the word as Black slang for a female. However, Vanzant cannot find a good use for *nigger*, but is able to redefine the word *bitch*. She says she really can't find anything affirming for the words *nigger* or *bitch*. Historically, Vanzant reminds the word *nigger* is "oppressive" as she "cannot find another energetic for it." Recalling a time not so long ago, just decades away, some segments of society "hung *niggers*" and others "raped *nigger* bitches"!

Many people from all walks of life have encountered the word in some way, shape, or form. Jarrett remembers her first conversation about race centered on the ugliness of this word. She remembers her first conversation on race with her daughter like it was yesterday. She says her daughter was in nursery school, the same school she attended when she was a kid. "She went into the bathroom" at the private school she was enrolled in. Her daughter attended the University of Chicago Laboratory School in a very progressive, integrated community. Two little girls called Jarrett's daughter a *nigger*, and one of them said, "Why do you have hair like that? Your hair is horrible." Jarrett recalled, "you are in the bathroom and you are five years old, four years old, that is a pretty traumatic experience. She came out and told the teacher, and the teacher called me. And first thing I thought about is, you can't be mad at the kids at that age. They did not hear those words on the playground. They heard those words at home. And to their credit, the parents of the children, moms all called me and apologized. But I remember thinking, don't ever get too comfortable, even in Hyde Park in Chicago, at this illustrious private school that is a progressive community. You are not safe anywhere. I had to sit down and really have a long talk with my daughter about why these girls said what they said and how her hair is beautiful and she is beautiful and you can't let what people say in any way affect you. But today if you ask her about the experience, she remembers it quite vividly."

As I referenced dictionary origins of the n-word, I found that it has been around for hundreds of years with a trajectory of hundreds more. There are times when the word was used to demean, relegate, and hurt people of African descent in this country. Marvie Darden, the mother of Christopher Darden, the former Los Angeles prosecutor in the O. J. Simpson trial, recalled to her son, specifically for this book, an incident around 1948 that is forever etched in her mind, even in her autumn years. Darden recalls from their December 31, 2015, New Year's Eve conversation the eighty-one-year-old Marvie Darden, mother of eight, told her son, "In school she had an argument with a White girl over a ball." The issue was, who had it first? Mrs. Darden set the scene of the school: "In school there were a few Indians, only a handful of Blacks, and hardly any Mexicans. The school was otherwise White."

Darden's mom told her attorney son, "The White teacher got involved and as she asked, 'Who started it?' A White student, whose name she still knows today, said, 'The *nigger* started it.' The teacher immediately sided with the White girl and without hearing her side took the ball and gave it to the White girl." The argument over the ball was because Mrs. Darden wanted to pitch, but the teacher would never let her. Mrs. Darden recalled that the Blacks "were very athletic but the White girl that always pitched was not very good." According to her, the little girl would walk the hitters, and her team always lost. Chris Darden said, "Mama asked for the ball" and decided she would pitch when the girl began to argue with her. The teacher walked up, and that's when the White boy said, "The *nigger* started it."

Mrs. Darden was called to the principal's office. She was mad because the White boy called her out of her name. When she complained to the principal, he ignored her but instead addressed only her conduct, starting an argument and taking the ball. She was held after school every day for a week. Darden said, "This angered Mama, but also created fear. That incident created a domino effect. After school the Black kids walked a few miles down the railroad tracks to the public housing where they lived called "The Canal." The walk was dangerous because of all the hobos that lived along the tracks. Every day she walked those tracks alone for a week because the other Black kids had already gone home."

Fast-forward to New Year's Eve, December 31, 2015, just hours before the stroke of midnight signaling feelings of hope and possibilities of change for the better with the refreshing of dates on the calendar to the new year of 2016. Early that morning Darden met with his elderly parents in California's Bay Area. He began a conversation about race specifically for this book project. To my surprise, Darden had never had this conversation with his parents before. He was intrigued to learn things he had not recalled hearing before. It was emotional for him hearing this from his mother as he realized they are in their golden years and he did not know this. Marvie Jean Darden was born in 1934. Darden says of his mother's childhood, she lived "in east Texas, Gilmer, there was segregation. But you could do stuff with White people, it just depended on the White people and who they were. Some didn't let them play with their kids, while others did. You could live across the road from White folks and they would not speak to you, depending on who those White folks were." But Marvie Jean moved when she was eight. Her family moved from Texas to California in 1942.

As things seemed to get better in race relations in this country, there still was no shortage in the use of the n-word. In the '60s the groundbreaking crime drama series *The Mod Squad* had its supporters and its share of detractors. The central cast consisted of two White people, a male and a female, and a Black man. Actor Michael Cole portrayed an undercover police officer in the show. He is a White man born in Madison, Wisconsin, in 1945. But when the Aaron Spelling series aired from 1968 to 1973, there was an uproar in response to certain scenes. Cole vividly remembers the hate mail the show received. "As far as *The Mod Squad* goes, most people had no idea of how much hate mail I got. For example, during one scene there was a full head close-up of Linc (Clarence Williams) in a very tense situation. Sweat was getting in Linc's eyes, so Pete reached in the frame with my White hand to wipe his brow with a piece of my torn shirt. Wow! The mail was about how could a White guy (me) mop the brow of a [n-word]?' When that kind of mail showed up, I knew we were on the right track. The three of us—Pete, Linc, and Julie—truly cared for each other, and that came across the television screen."

But the show was created to change hearts. "When I first met Aaron Spelling, I told him I thought the show was stupid and I hoped it never got on the air. Aaron said, 'Mick . . . that attitude is exactly what I want! This show will be about caring for each other,'" according to Cole.

When I listen to these and other stories, it further convinces me not to use the word. However, I am guilty like many others of having used this racist and demeaning word more times than I care to admit. No matter how it was used, in public or private, with the "a" or the "er," it was wrong. Moving forward, as Dr. Maya Angelou said, "Once you know better, you do better." As a mother who works to instill values in my children and others around me, I can't in good conscience utter the word. I am—and we are—far better than that. I cringe when I hear it in music, film, or out in public. I also cringe each time it is used in this book.

Yes, some African Americans do use the word, but that does not make it right. The evidence of that was clear on September 21, 2016, when boxing promoter Don King used a public platform to throw Black people under the bus while exalting Republican Party presidential candidate Donald J. Trump. With Donald Trump and others in attendance, both Black and White, smiling in anticipation of what he would say, Don King spoke of his conversation with singer Michael Jackson essentially saying that no matter what level you achieve, you are always a [n-word]. Come on! Anger and shame over what

Don King said does not even come close to describing the scope of emotions that boiled to the surface.

Join me in purposefully allowing the word to die! All of us, of all races, are better than this. Its origins come from hate and anger. I find it deplorable that it is embraced for any kind of good. Its embrace is a form of unconscious self-hate.

No more!

• 5 •

The Faith of Our Mothers

$\mathcal{T}$here is a sacred connection between race, religion, and mothers. When the dots of race are connected, the thread is strong, anchored by religion or some sort of call to a Higher Power, with motherhood and faith almost mimicking one another. In many instances, both these foundational categories, motherhood and faith, cross their own imaginary demarcation lines. They mirror one another in the tenderness of their love and the strength of their passion, no matter what the faith or the simplicity of moral value. The faith of our mothers is also about a mother's faith in the child she rears. AME Bishop Vashti McKenzie affirms the importance of a mother's love, particularly for children of color, enabling them [minority children] to "find their own value." She contends it is our God-given purpose as a mother to instill in them, "[Y]ou are valuable, you are worth it, you are somebody. The world will label you as nothing, as nobody, all of that, you're stupid, you're dumb, you are second place. People still have in their minds, 'This is all you can be. This is our expectation of you.' It is not just in business, it is in education, it is in community, it's in the people's family. We don't expect you to do that, and unless you prepare your children, they will live up to the expectation of the world. You have to raise your child."

My mother left this bit of motherly wisdom and advice that I found to be true as I walk the road of motherhood: a mother will stand with a child when the world forsakes them. These words remind me of how a mother offers so much to her child so he or she can make the best of their life that they can. The power of motherhood is spiritual, and quoting the Bible, "Children are a reward!"

I want to further emphasize the importance of mothers and their impact on children. Mothers impart more than thought. During the gestational and

65

child-bearing process, a woman is everything for the fetus inside her womb. Through those months of preparation, we are the warmth and the sustenance for that child. Just that process alone creates something higher for the responsibility of motherhood. And that bond and love makes us want to protect and help our children become the best they can be. There are some stories of parenting and motherhood that are not so pretty, but the beauty of appreciating and celebrating other cultures still arose from hurt and pain.

Up to now, I did not fully realize how tangible a mother's impact is on her children, but then I began to chronicle a mother's influences on decision making and actions when it comes to matters of race. At the core of this issue is how extremely personal matters of race can be, and in most cases they are an issue of the heart that dwells in the most spiritual of places. Therefore, a mother as nurturer has her emotional and substantive platforms. These offer the sometimes secret perspective that will help shape the next generation's navigation of society's race matters that are growing more complex. The complicated resolution of race problems in America is found deep inside the soul. I am reminded of something President Obama said on March 6, 2015, in the East Room at the *In Performance at the White House: Women of Soul* event. The forty-fourth President of the United States of America pronounced, not with his executive power, but to the crowd invited there to celebrate the richness of the African American spirit: "Ultimately that is what soul is all about, telling some truth!"

Racial attitudes and behaviors are making the "A" block of the nightly news and offering eye-catching headlines above the fold in mainstream newspapers. These modern-day racial conflicts are news-making, controversial, and well publicized as the national population is browning in color. The babies of color born today in the United States are a "majority minority." It is no longer a concept but reality that this nation will be majority minority in a few decades. In 2014, the US Census Bureau found there were more than twenty million children under five years old living in the United States, and 50.2 percent of them were minorities. Children whose parents identify them as White with Hispanic origin were the largest minority, making up 22 percent of the 19.9 million children under age five, followed by African American children, who make up 15 percent.

The article "10 Reasons You'll Love Living in a Majority-Minority America," by Roque Planas and Carolina Moreno, published May 7, 2015, confronts the argument of minority status in this nation by concluding:

> Without a numerically dominant race, people of every group could be more inspired to drop discriminatory biases and challenge the racial injustices that continue to define the American experience for many.

While I was covering the presidency of William Jefferson Clinton, he continually spoke of a nation that was browning. He offered a way to work through this very sensitive issue via the President's Initiative on Race. This program looked at ideas for legislation, but it ultimately narrowed it all to a heart issue, something we cannot legislate. Essentially, our hearts and minds have to be aligned to adequately legislate the issue, to effectively and substantively eliminate racial hate and injustice.

The racial division is still very real, with high numbers of negatives in almost every category in the Black community. Efforts to turn the tide have fallen on many hardened hearts. In my humble estimation, in many instances, past racial hurts and haunts can and do overshadow the attitudes and perceptions that trickle down to our children.

Sitting in the office of Georgia 5th District Congressman John R. Lewis, in the Cannon Office Building, I listened to his memories of his mother, Willa Mae Lewis, and her faith in God. The conversation unintentionally offered a spiritual witness to our time together. He discussed how her faith spoke to his spirit to help foster great equality and racial change in this country. John Lewis vividly recalled of his mother, how her calls to God reverberated through his spirit at a very young age.

Willa Mae Lewis, of Troy, Alabama, was a sharecropper, wife of a sharecropper, and the mother of ten, including a young, racially inquisitive John Robert Lewis. She was a woman who keenly understood the South and the condition of Black folks there. She learned, as a Black person in Alabama, "not to rock the boat," which was a necessity for survival, according to Congressman Lewis. Without detailing what she may have seen or been witness to, there was an unspoken understanding that she must have seen a lot when it came to race in the Deep South. But her ultimate goal was for her ten children, seven boys and three girls, to "get them grown." The meaning of this common Southern phrase in the Black community, is that a parent's hope is to safely raise children to adulthood. Then, depending on the home environment, at sixteen, seventeen, eighteen, or even twenty-one, the children are responsible for their own lives. This was also a time when kids married very young, moving into adulthood early.

Mrs. Lewis was God-fearing, putting all her trust in Him for all things, from the small to the large. Her faith even extended to calming the fears of one terrified child when storms arose. A young John Lewis did not perceive Mother Nature as being so kind and inviting with what he felt were her vicious Southern storms. These, Lewis recounted, set fire to fields, barns, and hay. A mother's firm faith comforted her child from those raucous sounds of the storms and deadly flashes of lightning that cracked the sky. As her son was terrified of the tempest, Mrs. Lewis's faith led her firmly to believe they would survive nature's fierce roar.

But her son, who withstood the bites of dogs and the skull-fracturing swing of billy clubs during the civil rights movement, needed his mom's protection from the storms then, and as she is no longer with us, he still enjoys remembering her comforting, calming presence even now. Believe it or not, this great man, who stood up to the ugliest of things, is still afraid of what Mother Nature offers in the way of thunder and lightning. He recalls how his mother would say during the storms, "Be quiet, be quiet, stop talking, the Lord is doing HIS work!" Many from the South were quiet during storms, revering the Lord and His mighty hand through Mother Nature's efforts to water her land. Mrs. Lewis's spiritual call for peace and calm during the storm draws on the biblical story of Jesus on the boat during a severe storm. Paraphrasing the scripture, Luke 8:22–25, "And his disciples were fearful when the storms arose while they were at sea. Jesus said, 'Peace, be still.' And there was calm."

There is a significant parallel between Mrs. Lewis and her faith calming her son's extreme fears and how he took that faith and marched on without fright in the American civil rights tsunami. He was trained for the clashes and always stood strong on the faith his mother practiced, that it would get him and the others through. Lewis recalls the storms of the civil rights period, during the '50s and '60s, saying, "Faith played a major role. Without faith, without hope, without grace we would not have survived, without love. It was this belief that somehow and someway, 'I got this from my mother,' God is going to take care of us. He will not let his children down."

Lewis also recalls from his childhood that they were very, very poor. "I would hear my mother moaning and singing while she was cooking, and she would say, 'I have never seen the righteous forsaken or his seed begging for bread.'" But, according to Lewis, "We kept on . . . to see what the end was going to be." Ultimately his mother's faith inspired him to press for a better day during his time at the Student Nonviolent Coordinating Committee (SNCC) and marching with Dr. King. All that while, she was not in agreement with her son.

Without acknowledging it, as Lewis told his stories about his mother, it was as if she relied on God to fix it all. As I ponder Congressman Lewis's story about his mother, she, a Black woman in Alabama, must have instinctively relied on God understanding in her soul, "Be still and let the Lord work." Meaning, my thought is, that she believed He alone would fix the racial injustices, and maybe that is why she would rebuff her son on matters of race when he asked questions about the condition of Blacks back in Troy, Alabama. His mother at the time did not want him interjecting himself into the process. But, as history shows, that's exactly what he did!

But John Lewis kept asking those questions about race of his God-fearing mother, a woman who did not talk much about the issue. Lewis recalls he would ask his mother "about the signs that said White and Colored" in 1954, '55, and '56. Lewis lovingly remembers, "My mother would say I was nosy and head hard." She was the one for him to ask, as he revered her so. Looking back on their time together, he acknowledged he was closer to his mother than his dad. She lived to the age of eighty-nine and would be one of the closest and most influential relationships of his life.

One memorable race discussion between Willa Mae Lewis and her young son, John Robert Lewis, came when she discovered he was working to make change in this country, particularly in the racist South. He was attending nonviolence workshops, taking part in sit-ins, and marching with Dr. King. He had never told her of his activist actions. But she found out. Her talk came in the form of a letter to her child when she discovered his attempts to attend the all-White Troy State.

Lewis remembers his family was "very poor," but his father, Eddie Lewis, had been able to purchase that land for $300. (The Lewis family still owns that land today.) Now, he fondly recalls his days working in the fields on the family farm, admitting he did not like the work and he was very "slow" doing his share. But after all that hard work to have a piece of the American Dream a Black man was allowed back then, it was in jeopardy.

The family was warned by Dr. King, if they proceeded in the quest for John to attend and become the first Black at Troy State, they could lose their 110 acres of land, and their house could possibly be bombed. Essentially, they could lose it all for the dreams of the young John Lewis. This was 1958.

As the young John Lewis was pressing for the mark of first-class citizenship for Blacks, his mother was not in support of this. There may be a clear explanation for Mrs. Lewis's attitude and for the other mothers'. They did not want their children on the front lines, almost making them the sacrificial lambs for our equality. President Obama's spiritual advisor, Joshua DuBois, the former head of the Obama administration's Faith-Based Initiative and the CEO of Value Partnerships, finds, "Mothers are the ones who have to bear the greatest burden of heartbreak, really. At the end of the day, when our people are enduring the things we have endured, it is the mothers that are the primary carriers of the emotional burden in that way. We have seen that from slavery to Reconstruction, and I would even say I am sure that mothers today from Trayvon Martin's mother to Michael Brown's mother have been at the forefront of these movements."

This movement, the civil rights movement, the most successful movement in this nation's history for change, did not have the support of the masses. Some doors were even closed to young people seeking liberty for all. At that time, a very small minority of churches supported the movement. Congressman Lewis affirmed what Black leaders have said: that only about 4 percent of Black churches supported Dr. King.

Fast-forwarding to 2015, Congressman Lewis recalls his mother finally jumped on the bandwagon in 1965 when the Voting Rights Act was passed. Willa Mae Lewis changed her stance on her son's involvement. It all stemmed from her faith that was transferred to her iconic son who felt, because his mother believed, that he should trust that God would carry the movement for civil rights through! This crescendo was from the efforts of her son and others when she did not want to buck the status quo of the South. But the irony was that her faith was pivotal for the movement.

> Honor your father and mother, that your days may be prolonged in the land which the LORD your God gives you. (Exodus 20:12)

Early on, young John Lewis, the son of Eddie and Willa Mae, held his mother in high esteem and gave her a gift no one had ever offered her before. It was something simple and, for many, a titling that is often taken for granted. A young, thoughtful John Lewis, as a boy, would at times preach to the chickens on the farm. He also began to offer his mother a title the White women in the town would get, a prefix to her name. He called her *Mrs.* Lewis. At a very young age he understood other women in his area were being called "Mrs.," but his mother was never offered that title by people, particularly White folks. They would address her by her name or by "Aunt Willa Mae," never "Mrs. Lewis." So in an effort to give his mother her recognition, he called her "Mrs. Lewis," to the amazement of others, like his aunts. His mother never complained about her special gift from her son.

During the conversation for this book, Congressman John Lewis recalled his days marching with Dr. King and how the countless numbers of women, including many "Mothers of the Movement," opened up their homes to the nonviolent demonstrators. Conditions may not have always been the best, but they appreciated every bit of help and made the best of the situation. Lewis singled out his friend, another icon, Harry Belafonte, offering him as an example of how they lived during the boycotts, marches, and nonviolent protests. Harry Belafonte and John Lewis sometimes roomed together in people's homes, as Blacks were not allowed to stay in many hotels, and if they could, the marchers couldn't afford it.

Lewis remembered, decades later, it was the mothers and countless other women, in many instances, who made their homes comfortable for the marchers and fed them with food from their fields. He says he couldn't imagine the movement without them.

> Faith is the substance of things hoped for and the evidence of things unseen. (Hebrews 11:1)

When we look at faith and motherhood, there is a correlation where both are centered on love, and they rely on a strength of passion. And when Lewis looks back at the women and mothers of the struggle, he says they were the "soul sisters before there were soul sisters." During that time it really did take a village to raise a child.

Belafonte and Lewis share that unique and strangely privileged past of marching and planning in the inner circle with Dr. King in the fight for equality. However, there is even more commonality in how they arrived at those pivotal moments. The hard knocks of life and watching a mother's personal and very apparent struggle helped mold Belafonte. "I was an activist in fact, who became an artist. They ask why did I become an activist, because I was Black, I lived in America, and because I was born in poverty. All those credentials at the time of birth motivated my mother and my family and everybody in my community to become engaged in trying to survive and to live in dignity and trying to live lives out that were worthy of us. And that was a huge struggle. And I watched my mother, as an immigrant woman, fight desperately to overcome inequities of justice and poverty."

He spoke with me by phone for a February 2016 interview where he announced his endorsement for presidential candidate Bernie Sanders. He said he is an activist and then an actor. Life facts circulated around his immigrant mother, who was affectionately called Millie. She emigrated from Jamaica, like her brothers and sisters, to the United States.

Melvine Bellafanti was part of the revolution in manufacturing in the 1920s. She raised her six children practically as a single parent, according to her oldest child, the almost ninety-year-old actor Harold George Bellafanti Jr., better known as Harry Belafonte. The world-renowned actor spoke in that melodic, raspy, distinctive voice I remembered from watching classic movies like *Carmen Jones*. He said of his real-life woes, "The burden of raising her children was on my mother, and she did it admirably."

Belafonte, with a quickness in his response, flowed with memories of his mother in New York. His recollections of his father are of "almost an absentee" parent, caught up in alcohol. Belafonte also used the word *brutal* in describing his dad. Without skipping a beat in his life story, he remembers that his activism germinated from the truth of his mother's life. "When I watched her struggle to make a life, to justify itself in her mind, I saw the struggle that she went through. I made a commitment to myself as a kid. If ever I had the opportunity to change the path we were on, I would commit myself to that eternally. It was an investment she made."

Harry Belafonte's mother's faith was in her son's spirit to move the mountains that were insurmountable for her at the time. He tells of before the family immigrated, "She once said to me when I saw her in a rather severe moment, no employment, no money, not knowing quite how to feed her children. She stared at the wall in our little one-room hut that we lived in. I asked her what was the matter, and she just said very simply, 'Harry, when you grow up, never, ever come up against an injustice you could have done something about and did not do it.' I understood it. And as daunting as that remark was, she said something that was indelible in my life."

His mother's request became truth for the entertainer after he entered the military and fought in World War II. Belafonte said when the movement started after the war, "I engaged in everything. I was with DuBois, Paul Robeson, with A. Philip Randolph, all through Harlem with Langston Hughes." Belafonte acknowledges, at that time, he was the youngest in the group as he listened to his "mentors." Belafonte affectionately remembers his mother, who lived into her late seventies.

The harsh realities of race have forever impacted Sybrina Fulton, the mother of Trayvon Martin. She contends that when it comes to matters of race in the United States, we need compassion. She is calling for the government to do more and for people to also consider the disparities that harshly affect minority populations as a heart issue. As it relates to the heart, Fulton emphasizes there is also a responsibility for "more religious sectors or more religious organizations getting involved." She calls out the bias when it comes to the victims of deadly violence, asserting, "The country needs more compassion," saying hurt and suffering is universal. "A lot of times people get caught up around, 'Was he Black or White?' 'Was he Hispanic?' It really does not matter, somebody has a loss. Somebody is hurting."

With everything she has been through, Fulton still considers herself an "average mom" as she continues to raise and nurture her surviving son, Jahvaris Fulton. At the same time, she's working to heal from the fatal shooting death of her son, seventeen-year-old Trayvon, in 2012. Sybrina Fulton is reaching out to help other Black mothers who lost their kids from similar tragedies cope with their lives. Even as poised as she has been through it all, the death of her son and the trial of the man who killed Trayvon, she still hurts.

Sybrina Fulton has dug deep in her pain. She has used her compassion to create an organization called The Circle of Mothers. She says, "I just don't think I am ever going to get past losing my son so tragically and suddenly. That is a chapter in my life. I don't care how old I get, I still have that chapter in my life."

The Circle of Mothers helps the mothers of loss cope by embracing what happened and trying hard to find the next step.

As the mother of a boy, Rae Dawn Chong has her own thoughts on motherhood and teaching children about race: "Well, today you can die being Black, just standing, somewhere in public, you can die. That is ridiculous and tragic and very wrong, and I know that if White children, men and boys, and women were suffering like this, there would be massive change immediately. I know there is change occurring, but it isn't severe enough or fast enough and I still think a deep cleansing of all our government agencies must happen. We cannot hire White nationalists as policemen, and something tells me that memo went out and every skinhead who could, is a cop. If they are not cops, they are judges. We need to rout them out immediately. The entire police force in Chicago, for instance, is scary to me. It is a countrywide problem. I would tell all the brown babies of every race to be cautious and to be mindful and respectful, and if necessary never travel alone and to record any and all altercations. Because in America, they are not safe. Period."

At the end of the day, motherhood is a spiritual experience. You are selfless in your love and support, completely giving of yourself for the good of the child. Your talks and efforts to help chart a course for another person are one of the most wonderful of experiences. However, when race interjects itself in one of its ugliest forms, it takes the strength of a Higher Power to get through. That is when the sisterhood of mothers really plays a part.

★ ★ ★

In the fall of 2015, former Secretary of State Hillary Clinton met with a group of Black mothers hit by racist tragedy since 2012. Hillary Clinton is no stranger to issues of race, not just because she has been in political life for decades, but also because she was raised to accept differences.

Clinton learned, from her own mother's hard life experiences, that every life is precious. She remembers her mother being "adamant that we treated everybody with respect and dignity." Clinton recalls her mother's personal story, saying, "She was abandoned by her parents and grandparents." The former First Lady, Secretary of State, and as this is being written, Democratic Party presidential candidate, said her mother "had a really miserable childhood." Clinton remembers her mother, Dorothy, was able "to avoid bitterness and breakdown because people were kind to her."

Dorothy Emma Howell Rodham's mind and heart were open and inclusive as a result of hurt, "rejection," and "abandonment" from her White mother, and White grandparents, due to family dysfunction and divorce. At the age of fourteen, Dorothy Howell learned the hard life lessons of survival. She was a "housemaid" by day, cleaning houses and going to school. These stories reverberate with shocking similarities and reflections of my own family tree.

(I could not help wonder about Hillary Clinton's mother's life. Just months after my interview with her, I found out about my own maternal grandmother. She was reared by a sickly aunt. By day my grandmother, then a young girl in the south, went to her one-room schoolhouse, and when she returned, she worked in her aunt's home, helping out around the house.)

During the annual Congressional Black Caucus Legislative Week, mid-September 2015, I conducted an exclusive phone interview with Hillary Clinton. She reflected on her mother, a Sunday school teacher who had a lot of hard life lessons. She said that when her mother was a little girl, God was an important part of her life. Clinton said that her mother's "favorite childhood hymn was 'Jesus Loves the Little Children of the World.'" Hillary Clinton believes that song is an explanation of her mother's life story.

Dorothy Rodham found it in her heart to appreciate another culture and may have even found commonality with another ethnic group in America. However, she and her new friends sometimes found themselves unwanted—by a very vocal group of mainstream Americans. According to her proud daughter Hillary, a very young Dorothy Rodham "grew up in California at a time when there was a lot of prejudice against Japanese Americans, and she made really good friends, when she was in high school, with Japanese Americans. That was her first introduction to overcoming stereotypes and prejudice."

The 1930s in California for Dorothy Rodham was a time when there were large enclaves of Japanese immigrants. Subsequently, in 1942, the year Dorothy Howell married Hugh Rodham, World War II was raging. That, of course, deeply impacted the lives of Japanese Americans. About 120,000 Japanese Americans were taken and held in internment camps because of a fear that their loyalties were with their ancestral homeland. This was all done under an executive order from President Franklin D. Roosevelt.

Along with close relationships with Japanese Americans, the former Secretary of State remembers her mother grew up meeting people from all walks of life. But when Hillary Rodham was born, they resided in an "all-White suburb of Chicago, at the time." Also at that time Hugh Rodham had a small business where they used "day laborers who were predominately African Americans." Mrs. Clinton recalls, "My father and my mother worked with those men and one in particular, they tried to support his dreams and his family."

Clinton, once a Goldwater Republican, credits her embrace of racial difference to her "mother's experiences, the practical experience in my home, and my church's teachings." When Hillary Rodham was fourteen, her church's youth minister asked the youth group if they wanted to attend an event in Chicago where Dr. Martin Luther King Jr. was speaking. Clinton emphasized, during our book interview, how some of the parents of the kids in that church youth group "would not give their children permission" to attend the King event. At that time, Dr. King was traveling the country, working hard to garner support to change the racist system to an integrated society where all Americans could live first class. Clinton proudly remembers her mother's immediate words about the event. According to Hillary, Mrs. Rodham emphasized, "He is a great man. He is trying very hard to end the way people who are Black are treated. I want you to go hear him for yourself." With delight Clinton says of her mom, "My mother was a strong advocate for what the civil rights movement represented, and I am grateful every day that she was."

This interview was conducted during the time Clinton was working to become the forty-fifth president of the United States. And she recalled a sermon at the Foundry United Methodist Church, September 13, 2015, just weeks prior to our interview, which focused on Paul. The scriptural text was Romans 12. Her interpretation was that this was where the apostle Paul showed the marks of being a true Christian. She was clear in her conversation that she wanted to work with people of good faith as president to stop the divisions in this country.

I can't help but think of words from the book of James. James 2:17 spells it out, "Faith without works is dead." Those words meld the social and biblical message to remove the obstacles and impediments. For this moment it's racism. This is a practical approach, to use the Bible as the example to begin the evolution of racial change. This allows for confidence to stand against racist attitudes and behaviors that have yet to be slaughtered.

★ ★ ★

Maryland Congressman Elijah Cummings reflects on his mother's formula to combat racial intolerance during his childhood and youth. Cummings thinks of his mother's tangible approach. "She always had a way of trying to make us understand that we would be treated differently than White folks." Mrs. Cummings raised seven children, including little Elijah, whom she considered her protector. She tried to make it clear to her children that "We did not do anything wrong or we weren't less than anyone. But that it was White folks' problem. It was their way of putting us down so they could lift themselves up."

Congressman Cummings remembers how his mother worked to keep him from being "depressed" over the racial situation, telling her children they "had to work 10 times harder . . . by turning a negative, racism, and turning it into a positive and doing our very, very best and proving our greatness. That is one of the greatest gifts she has given me, that and my introduction to religion."

For Cummings, remembering his childhood comes with images of hurt from the racial divides that he questioned as a child. He wondered why, when he was around the age of seven or eight, Black people attended a small school and Whites had a larger schoolhouse. There were also stark differences in his shopping experiences. He recalls his mother's faith helped them cope with harsh life realities.

Cummings remembers when he raised these questions, his mother would respond, "Lord forgive them for they know not what they do." Those were the words Jesus used while on the cross before his death.

When Congressman Cummings's mother would use those powerful words, he did not understand fully what they meant, and he felt she was being too nice. He contends that when she would use this Bible scripture for that scenario, "I thought to myself, 'You damn straight they know what they are doing.' As I got older I understood what she was trying to say."

About ten years ago, Cummings, still a powerhouse leader on Capitol Hill, wanted to revisit some of the issues of his childhood. So he asked his mother what she meant by saying those words. Mrs. Cummings said, "Some people don't realize until it is too late."

But even as she would sing songs and consistently proclaim God out loud while doing her household chores, *"I have never seen the righteous forsaken or his seed begging for bread," (Psalms 37:25)*, she created a witness in her son, who felt a calling to help create a better day "for the least of these."

Cummings said his mother would use as an example of racial hate Alabama Governor George Wallace, who was vehemently against the civil rights movement in the 1960s and 1970s. Cummings recalls his mother's explanation: "Towards the end of his life, he [George Wallace] started saying things like 'I shouldn't have done that. I shouldn't have stood in the door of people trying to get into the University of Alabama.'"

Wallace, a four-time governor of Alabama who ran for president of the United States four times, wielded a lot of power and could have swayed folks in the opposite direction if he had had the epiphany decades earlier. He was elected governor of his state for the first time in 1962 with this declaration: "I draw the line in the dust and toss the gauntlet before the feet of tyranny, and I say, segregation now, segregation tomorrow, segregation forever."

But Cummings said of the conversation with his mother, "The damage had already been done. He [Wallace] had changed the trajectory, in a negative way, of so many Black folks' destiny. And so what she was trying to say, a lot of people, at the moment when they are doing these things, they are caught up in the moment, caught up in the crowd, caught up in racist dealings . . . and if they really believe in this God who sees all of us as equal . . . then they could not treat their brother, Black persons, the way they did."

But faith in some instances is not just about religion but a belief in a better day by being our better selves, where we treat others as we would like to be treated. It is the moral issue of this modern age, as religion and faith play a unique role in the dynamics of race. We quote the scripture: "Do unto others as you would have them do unto you" (Matthew 7:12).

But when we look with a microscope, this scripture is not as openly practiced as one would think. Teach them how to treat you! An example of this was during the highly publicized antics by Republican Congressman Darrell Issa. During a meeting of the House Oversight Committee, when Congressman Cummings tried to speak, Issa ended the meeting (more about this in Chapter 10).

The moral imperative or drive to do what is right has led many Americans, especially mothers and mother figures, to change the racial dynamic simply because the issue is just, fair, and proper. Cindy Williams, the costar of the TV show *Laverne and Shirley*, and author of the book *Shirley I Jest*, remembers her mother never had *the* race discussion, but Frances Williams led by example in how people should be treated. It was the moral imperative that came through. Williams says, "I never had a sit-down discussion with my mother about race. There was never any need for it, because in my early childhood we lived in my grandmother's house on Poplar Street in Dallas, Texas. And when I was five, we became the only White family living on the street. All the kids played together, and I remember my mother saying she never had such nice neighbors."

Cindy acknowledged that her mother's actions, not her words, "really made me blind to color. It gave me a natural and unshakable acceptance of everyone."

The generations in the Williams family kept with the same tradition when it came to conversations on race. She looks back on how she raised her own daughter on issues of the racial divide in the United States, saying, "I never had to sit down and talk to my children about race or color. Because of my life in entertainment, they grew up in a very colorful environment. My children take people as they come. They are empathic souls and see no color."

Cindy recalls when her daughter was six or seven around 1989 or 1990: "When my daughter was in the first grade, the class was taken to see *Anne of Green Gables*. I went along as room mother. There were over a thousand kids packed into the theater from all over the LA Unified School District. The curtain went up. The children were excited and mesmerized. The play was marvelous. None of the children saw any color, even though Anne was played by a Black actress, her mother, Asian, and her father, White. They just saw Anne and her family. It was a magnificent thing to behold."

★ ★ ★

The seventy-year-old actor Michael Cole, one of the stars of the groundbreaking TV crime drama *The Mod Squad*, looked back at his mother's influences on him and how she shaped the thoughts that led to his being part of this show.

The Mod Squad was not necessarily accepted by all people in this country when it came to having a prominent Black actor as a star character on TV, alongside White actors and actresses.

Cole boldly states, "Ma [Kathleen Hyland Cole] said she felt if there really is a 'DIFFERENCE' in the spirit of human life, the act of producing a child wouldn't work. Somehow, the spirits of 'all' the races work quite well with each other. When given a chance, the soul is the color of all of us."

Cole was born in 1945, in Madison, Wisconsin. Even as he is White, there was a difference for him being Catholic at that time in this country. He said, "I was brought up Irish Catholic. I never knew my biological father because he abandoned us when I was born. Ma never said too much about race. Not even when I was a child and saw a picture of a Black crucifix and asked her about it. She smiled and said, 'It makes no difference. All races are an act of God.'"

Cole also acknowledges her humanity: "Ma had a profound sense of fairness about all life, human or otherwise, especially about the poor or neglected. She also had a logical side to her thinking. She didn't talk about race much as she suggested to me to think about geography and race. The closer people are to the equator, and thousands of years in the sun, the pigment of their skin would become darker to protect the body from the more-intense ultraviolet rays from the sun. It made sense to me. Thanks, Ma, for the insight, spiritual or logical, they both worked for me. . . . For me, it all goes back to Ma and the 'no difference' between the Black or White crucifix."

★ ★ ★

For me, when it came to issues big or small and racial or nonracial, my mother, the late Mary Vivian Gowans Ryan, a woman of strong faith, always found the meaning in everything. She was a Sunday school teacher and a mentor and second mom to thousands of kids she worked with in her day job at Morgan State University.

But no matter her efforts, it was about her faith in her children, her girl and her boy, that she birthed and the other children she adopted along the way. It was about continuing to move forward, no matter the obstacle, because God was a clear and ever-present help. She always told me to keep going and never let anything get in my way. She was a woman who carried everything to God in prayer in her home, at church, or even stopping by a hospital chapel weekly to pray. She always told me God hears your cries. And He did. Even on her deathbed, she taught me elegance and courage and faith as she knew she was dying.

It has taken me a long time to publicly share these details, but she was a mother until the end. She told everyone she had three months to live, and I was the last person she told because we were so close. I don't know where the strength came from, but I stood with her every step. Yes, my dad and my brother stood too, but I was able to fill in the gap for them when they couldn't. I was working at the White House as the American Urban Radio Network White House correspondent and Washington Bureau chief. I was also pregnant with my second child. My mother told people around her that she was not afraid to die, but she wanted to see her grandchildren grow. She had just had a grandbaby, my brother's daughter, and could not see the child because of her illness, leukemia. My niece Ella is a reflection of my mother just like my oldest child Ryan. And just 7 months later, my mother's last grandchild, Grace, was born.

My mother watched my stomach grow during the first six months of my pregnancy, just after she had been diagnosed. She was a grandparent to my oldest daughter until Ryan was 5 years old and then death took my mother away from us. Even in that short window of time, Ryan knew her grandmother loved her. She had my mother wrapped around her finger. My mother would insist on buying her granddaughter things like most grandmothers do. Also during those last few difficult months, she and I had a chance to have many heart-to-heart, very real talks. I told Mommy, as I affectionately called her even as an adult, "I may not have been the child you wanted, but I love you." She said to me, "Who ever told you that? I love you!"

She let me know I was everything she ever hoped for and more. To my surprise, though, she didn't understand where I got my will to fight, as she was such a classy, graceful and elegant woman. But she loved and admired my determination.

We did not know at the time if she would beat this cancer or if she would succumb. She prayed and read her Bible and talked with me and her immediate family members. I was hoping against hope and praying she would live, but God saw fit to bring her home to Him. Just hours before she passed, I said, "I love you," and she told me, "I love you back!" After I left, my dad, in disbelief, stayed in that room. My mother had told me to go home, as she knew she would transition from this world that night. She died early that morning, and before they wheeled her out of her hospital room at Johns Hopkins Hospital, we had a religious service for her. We sang to God and praised Him for His mighty hand and allowing her to be in our lives. We quoted scripture. I have never fully opened up about that time. Now, more than nine years later, I can. My life has changed drastically since then, but because of my mother's faith in God and in me, I can face it all. I am thankful she was allowed to be my mother!

After my mother died, I unknowingly began looking at my life, the ups and downs, in the way that she did. That God was always trying to show me the meaning of something that had happened or was going to happen. When it came to race, she would tell me her stories but always ended with, "That was then, and look at us now." She was a firm believer in a better day but very cognizant of the past, always believing things were getting better. Since her death nine years ago, I just wonder what she would say today.

She was part of a team, with my father, but she was the nurturer, the one we went to with our hurts. She was soft in her approach and wisdom but strong in her faith in us, praying and reading the Bible all the time. But she always encouraged, in all ways, both my brother and me, in our endeavors, he in his business and me in broadcasting and with my books. She taught us that with hard work we could be anything or do anything that we set our minds to. I still live by that motto and instill it in my children. Also, as the big sister, when I see my brother's steps not as sure and deliberate as they could be, I remind him of who he is and of our mother's words. It was and still is her faith in God and in us that makes my day better. Thanks, Mommy!

But at the end of the day, Bishop Vashti McKenzie summed it up best when it came to saving our kids from the world, particularly mothers and their children of color having to "conspire" to keep them safe.

★ ★ ★

Was it the time or the circumstances that fostered the rise of a crop of determined people in the 1950s and '60s who stood for racial equality and against the accepted practice of second-class citizenship for Blacks in this country? No matter the answer, in a number of family settings a mother played a role in some way in shaping attitudes about racial matters. Many families with differing backgrounds and life experiences felt similar impacts from a mother's words and actions in shaping attitudes toward the call for justice and equality.

My mother, Vivian Ryan, pregnant with me, sitting beside my father, Robert, and her friend, Mavis.

Vivian Ryan receives the award for April being the winner of the NAACP Baby Contest for her church.

Younger years. An early birthday with both of my parents, Robert and Vivian, helping unwrap birthday gifts in our apartment in Northwest Baltimore.

Mother and daughter share a seat at a family event. My mother loved putting my hair up in what she called "a bush ball."

Baltimore in the 1990s. Mother's Day was always big in our family. I was working that day for a local radio station, where we celebrated the day so I wouldn't miss out. Shown in the photo are Robert Ryan Jr., Vivian Gowans Ryan, the author, and Robert Ryan Sr.

Me and my mother Vivian Gowans Ryan in August 2015 at Brown University in Rhode Island celebrating a friend's wedding.

Wedding day.

My 39th birthday. The last birthday party I celebrated with my mother. I thought I was turning 40. She said I always wanted to be older than I actually was.

Me and my daughter Ryan with the Obamas at Christmas.

Me and my daughter Grace with the Obamas at Christmas.

Ryan hangs with President Obama during a game at Towson State University where his brother-in-law was coaching the opposing basketball team.

The girls meet the first president I ever covered as a White House reporter. Shown in the photo are President Bill Clinton, the author, Ryan, and Grace.

Special moments together. In March 2016 we traveled to the kids' favorite city, New York, as Ryan was part of her school choir group singing at Carnegie Hall.

November 2016, a day off from school for the girls. We are in the Rose Garden at the White House watching the turkey being pardoned by President Barack Obama.

The London Eye, London, England, June 2016. The author with her two daughters, Ryan and Grace.

The summer of 2014 readying for our first canoe ride together, with Ryan and Grace in Maryland.

My mom meets President Bill Clinton.

· *6* ·

Mothers, Presidents, and Race

I am one of a small number of people who have the privilege of being the first line of questioning of an American president. I cover everything from war to peace and all things in between. And I often wonder about these national leaders as people and what makes them tick. As I am a mother myself, reflecting on my mother's wisdom, I wonder what advice these men were given by their mothers, particularly on race. That advice includes what their mothers said to them before, during, and after the Oval Office. With only forty-four members, most deceased, the presidency is an ultra-exclusive club that offers very little insight into the thinking of these men. It is no surprise that I've wanted to find out more about the presidents, particularly on matters of race in America.

My curiosity was piqued during a March 2016 news interview with Congressman James Clyburn of South Carolina. He gave me a glimpse into the mind-set of the mother of one of the antisegregation presidents, Harry Truman. President Truman's mother was against his landmark Executive Order 9981, desegregating the US military. The executive order established the President's Committee on Equality of Treatment and Opportunity in the Armed Services, committing the government to integrating the military. This meant the Colored and White units, which were completely separate from one another, were now joined.

Clyburn firmly believes that when you rank US presidents, Harry Truman should be in the top three. Clyburn believes that fighting the stain of racism was the barrier against Truman's receiving the accolades he deserved. Clyburn feels that "the reason he [Truman] was not considered a great president when he left office is what he did on behalf of Black folks. It was all about him integrating the Armed Services."

A dissenting voice came from an unlikely corner. Truman's mother was on the same side as the large portion of America that was against integration. Clyburn affirmed, "His [Truman's] own mother chastised him for what he did!" It all centered on the executive order. Clyburn stated, "Truman issued an executive order because Congress would never do it."

George W. Bush issued more executive orders than Barack Obama has, but executive orders are not the only kind of presidential actions issued by the forty-fourth president. Today, when there is constant political gridlock in Congress, President Obama has chosen to issue both crucial executive orders and executive memoranda, to the consternation of the opposing party. Both sides of Pennsylvania Avenue debate these actions at every turn. But it is certain now that President Truman's Executive Order 9981 was on the right side of history.

Clyburn reminds us there was another society-altering executive order, from President Abraham Lincoln, that "freed the slaves" on January 1, 1863. The Emancipation Proclamation declared, "All persons held as slaves within any State or designated part of a State, the people whereof shall then be in rebellion against the United States, shall be then, thenceforward and forever free."

The National Archives has a letter, dated July 31, 1863, from Hannah Johnson, mother of a Northern Black soldier, written to President Lincoln. Hannah Johnson offers to President Lincoln, "When you are dead and in Heaven, in a thousand years that action of yours will make the ages sing your praises."

And indeed they do. In 2016, Reince Priebus affirmed, "We [Republicans] are the party of open equality, freedom, opportunity, Lincoln. We are the part of the Civil Rights Act. You don't know about it because we don't talk about it."

★ ★ ★

When it comes to race and presidents, there are stories of the Black women, to include Black mothers, who played significant activist roles against some of the worst ills inflicted upon the Black community. These Black women "change agents" were employed by Madam C. J. Walker and her hair care empire. Encouraged by Walker to be politically active, the women came together in what has been termed "beauty shop politics" at annual national Walker conventions and in their own home kitchen salons that were just as common for Black women as the storefront beauty shops.

A'Lelia Bundles, journalist, author, historian, and great-great granddaughter (via adoption) of Madam C. J. Walker, found her ancestor's empire was not just about employing thousands of people and promoting "healthy hair" for Black women, but that Walker was also "a political and social activist." Bundles contends she was "a race woman contributing money to the

NAACP's Anti Lynching Fund, speaking out very militantly on behalf of Black soldiers who were fighting in France during World War I, and advocating for women's economic independence." Bundles says Madam C. J. Walker's activism was evident in the role she played as a member of the committee that organized the massive Silent Protest Parade in New York after the July 1917 East St. Louis riots. Along with several Harlem leaders, Walker traveled to the White House to present a petition signed by Walker, W. E. B. DuBois, James Weldon Johnson, Fred Moore, and others urging President Woodrow Wilson to support legislation to make lynching a federal crime.

In the nineteenth and twentieth centuries, lynchings were very commonplace and on flagrant public display. This atrocity was in some cases advertised in newspapers for the community to see. Unfortunately, lynchings continued through the 1960s. The vast majority of lynchings in this nation were of Black people. But when it comes to the lynchings of Black people in this country, Bundles contends that they were "the #BlackLivesMatter issue of that era."

Madam C. J. Walker's petition was handed to a top White House staff member, not directly to President Woodrow Wilson, who was known to refuse to meet with Black leaders and promoted segregation in the military and federal employment. President Wilson also refused to publicly denounce lynchings.

Many modern-day Americans like to recall Ronald Reagan's history and proclaim him as one of the greatest presidents. He was known not to have the most favorable impression of the vast majority of Black America, despite his upbringing. His record is evident, as he was against the Civil Rights Act of 1964 and tried to weaken the Voting Rights Act of 1965. As president, Reagan did not support sanctions against South African apartheid. He talked of the welfare system being a poverty trap as he worked toward "welfare reform," and he used the pejorative phrase "welfare queen" starting in his 1976 campaign for the presidency. Also, as president, Reagan did not support the federal observance of the Martin Luther King holiday, even as he signed its observance into law.

But Reagan's early years were those of parents teaching him differently. The Miller Center, a nonpartisan affiliate of the University of Virginia, chronicles Ronald Reagan's early history with his mother, Nelle, and his father, Jack Reagan. Their actions as a family were based on their moral attitudes. Ronald Reagan's mother was an "active member of the Disciples of Christ" and his father was Catholic. They despised the KKK, particularly because of his father's religion. In the former president's autobiography, *An American Life*, Reagan spoke of how his mother was "color-blind" and encouraged him to bring Black football players home with him. The book also revealed that his brother's best friend was Black.

The Miller Center says Jack Reagan "[was] fiercely opposed to racial and religious intolerance. He refused to allow his children to see the film *Birth of a Nation*, because it glorified the Ku Klux Klan." However, as an adult seeking the highest office of the land, his actions may be seen as a contradiction to his parents' teachings. That noteworthy difference was evident in 1980. Ronald Reagan's first stop for his general election campaign for the Oval Office was Neshoba County, Mississippi. Neshoba County became known because of the ugliness that occurred there in the 1960s. It is the historic site of the murders of civil rights workers James Chaney, Andrew Goodman, and Michael Schwerner in June 1964. And shortly before those horrific murders, Neshoba County was the site of another racist attack, where members of the Ku Klux Klan had firebombed a Black church and beaten the terrified worshipers.

Fast-forwarding to today, I asked two of the living past presidents about their mothers and matters of race. Former President Jimmy Carter was gracious enough to offer these answers to my questions. His answers spoke volumes, as his mother led by example.

The ninety-one-year-old Jimmy Carter, who served one term as the thirty-ninth president, says of his mother, "I don't remember a conversation about race with my mother, Lillian Carter, when I was a small child. As a teenager my mother, a registered nurse, spent much of her time caring for sick African American people (all our neighbors) in our rural community. She had twenty-hour duty, where she stayed with the family from 2 a.m. until 10 p.m. each day. We children saw her rarely, except between her assignments. She treated all of them as equals, without preaching about it."

As he got older, Jimmy Carter saw more evidence of his mother's action, saying, "When I was an adult and returned home from my service on submarines, she was outspoken to all her family when a question arose about the equality of all people and the need for an end to racial segregation in our country. All of us children followed her counsel and her example, despite boycotts of our business and physical abuse of her grandchildren at school. In 1964, when Lyndon Johnson was running for president and was very unpopular in our area because of his promotion of civil rights, she volunteered to be his county campaign manager. Quite often, her automobile was covered in obnoxious graffiti, but she seemed to relish the disapproval of racists. There were never any long statements to us from my mother. Her lifetime of action set an unequivocal example for those around her."

Lillian Carter did not flinch and/or waver in who she was as a person promoting equality. Former President Carter said, "Later, she was known throughout our community as almost uniquely liberal on the race issue, but was immune and impervious to any implied criticism." And there was one thing she absolutely did not tolerate. With nine decades behind him, Jimmy

Carter recalls, "She condemned the use of the 'N' *word* in her presence among her peers, and forbade its use by any of us."

A younger president of a different generation, the first mixed-race president, who is officially labeled as the nation's first Black president, Barack Hussein Obama has a different view of that word. President Obama was asked this question prior to Larry Wilmore's comments at the White House Correspondents' Association dinner. The president said, "America's original sin of slavery casts a long shadow. And our more recent past—stained by Jim Crow and other forms of discrimination—is something we carry with us. We are not cured of bias or bigotry or even racism. And so, to focus on one word or another, no matter how hateful, misses the bigger point. It's not just a matter of it being impolite to say any particular word in public. That's not how we measure whether racism still exists, because the truth is bigotry and bias come in many different forms. Sometimes it's overt racism. We all know what that looks and sounds like. But prejudice is often unspoken. It's often the result of unconscious biases. So when we talk about where we've been and where we need to go to, it's important that our conversation be worthy of the subject matter. I'm less interested in a debate over a word than I am on keeping up the steady beat of progress—and continuing the march."

President Obama's perspectives, no less, were formed from his life and the experiences he has had. Those experiences were shaped by his mother, Stanley Ann Dunham. She, like my mother, was born in 1942. At the age of eighteen, in 1960, a White American, Stanley Dunham, married a Black Kenyan, Barack Obama Sr. This was a time when interracial marriage was still illegal in many states. Months later, she delivered her mixed-race son, Barack Hussein Obama. But even at such a young age, the future-president's mother understood the unique position they were both placed in. Just a year after the birth of their baby, Mr. and Mrs. Obama split. Yet President Obama's mother wanted to make sure he understood his history, both White and Black.

President Obama recalls, "When I was growing up, my mother would come home with books on the civil rights movement, and I read the speeches of Dr. King. She told me stories of Black schoolchildren in the South who didn't have the same chance at success as White schoolchildren, but who still became doctors and lawyers and scientists. It was in this context that I learned that to be Black was to shoulder an important burden. We know bigotry still exists—my mother knew that too—but we would betray the efforts of those who fought so hard for equality if we denied the possibility of progress and gave up. More than a single conversation with my mother, it was her love throughout my life that helped me see the world's promise, and inspired the best in me. I learned the value of not letting despair turn into cynicism—because it's hope that creates the change that we seek."

Before her death due to uterine and ovarian cancer at the age fifty-two, Stanley Ann Dunham lived in five states and three countries, all the while exposing her son to many cultures and life lessons that the average White or Black child typically does not experience. In 1992 after a more than 1,000-page dissertation, Stanley Ann Dunham became Dr. Dunham, obtaining her Ph.D. in anthropology. Using his mother's example and his unique position as a platform, President Obama offered recommendations for mothers in teaching future generations to navigate the often choppy waters of race.

President Obama said, "Well, this isn't just an issue for mothers to discuss. Fathers need to have these conversations, too. But in too many communities and too many homes where they are needed most, dads are not around. We need to change that. In our house, Michelle and I encourage these types of conversations with Sasha and Malia, because even if they haven't experienced exactly what we are talking about—or what's on the news—giving them the opportunity to reflect on their own hidden biases or stereotypes can be enlightening. We want to make sure that our two daughters know their heritage in all of its strengths and all of its struggle, mindful that their ancestors were both slaves and slave owners.

"We started the discussion early so our girls would be familiar with the world we live in and have a safe space to question it. The best part of being their dad, especially as they've grown up, is hearing their thoughts on the world and their take on so many of these issues. In many ways, their generation is a step ahead of us. It just doesn't make sense to my girls and their friends that anyone should be treated differently because of their race or gender or because of who they love. That's what makes me so optimistic about our future.

"The thing I want my daughters and every child in America to understand, and something I stress in the My Brother's Keeper initiative, is that they belong. From the Oval Office, to running a tech company, to teaching a class or doing research in a science lab, these places are within reach—every opportunity is open to them. That limitless sense of possibility, even in the face of real odds, is what makes this country great. And even as we reaffirm that progress takes time and there is work left to be done, we need to reassure our children that they are loved and valued, and can do anything—irrespective of what they hear or see in the world. The conversations don't need to be lectures, and they don't need to wait for a negative incident—every day, we can give our kids the tools to feel confident navigating their own way through life."

· 7 ·

A Tale of Two Cities

$\mathscr{B}$altimore is like many other urban centers. When you get into the weeds of looking at the construct of cities, there is at least one common denominator connecting cities throughout this nation and even the world. These are the varying socioeconomic communities that uniquely make up each locale. Like Baltimore, many cities, no matter if they're organically created or planned, have these differing sections that create flavor and authenticity.

The City of Baltimore is an area of pockets. They are examples of its polar opposite neighborhood dynamic. Take the Sandtown Winchester neighborhood in the Penn-North section of Baltimore. This is a place of extreme poverty, where the riots took place in April 2015. But when you move not far from that area, just blocks away to the enclave of Bolton Hill, there's wealth and status. There is a marrying of two worlds, but the twain shall never meet.

For a bit of background, in the 1980s under Kurt Schmoke, then mayor of Baltimore, $130 million was poured into that area in collaboration with the Rouse Company. This is the same company that in 1967 helped create Columbia, Maryland, a planned community that has been consistently ranked in the top ten best places to live and located in Howard County, one of the wealthiest counties in the nation. But once the new mayor, Martin O'Malley, ran City Hall, the steam on that project began to fade until it was no longer visible.

Baltimore, a working-class, blue-collar city, has recently been in the glaring spotlight, targeting the worst. There are families in the city and surrounding conjoined areas that send their kids to some of the most elite educational institutions in the country. They live in mega homes with an unparalleled lifestyle many people can only dream about. But Baltimore is bleeding. The wounds are open and exposed. Blight is a huge problem in the city, exacerbated by the loss of manufacturing jobs and globalization that gave Bethlehem

Steel the chance to leave. It was an employer that gave middle-class incomes to workers who did not have college degrees. There was a large group of people in Baltimore living the American Dream, with maybe a high school degree. When Beth Steel left town, unlike the Baltimore Colts on that snowy night in a Mayflower van, the city's hurt worsened.

Maryland Congressman Elijah Cummings was born in Baltimore. His laundress mother and sharecropping father had moved there from Manning, South Carolina, for a better life. They were particularly focusing on a better education for their expanding family. Cummings, who lives just blocks from Penn and North Avenues, one of the flash points of the Baltimore riots, says, "Baltimore, if we were honest with ourselves . . . reminds me of somebody who has a facial feature they don't like and refuses to look in the mirror because they don't want to see it." The problems were not a secret but were exposed in the glaring light of the media during the April 2015 youth-led riots.

Cummings acknowledges, "Baltimore, I think, is finally trying to squint to see that we have to improve our schools, that they are not what they need to be, particularly for African American children. That we have to improve our recreational activities because our children have nothing to do. Most importantly we have to improve the job situation, and prepare people for those jobs. We have to figure out ways to attract jobs to the City of Baltimore. . . . Those are Baltimore scars."

For Black Baltimore, the bloodletting began decades ago. April 4, 1968, is one of those vivid memories that millions share, globally. It was the day Dr. Martin Luther King Jr. was fatally shot on a balcony of the Lorraine Motel in Memphis, Tennessee. The drum major for justice, the man who championed the efforts for social and legal equality in this country, was killed.

Beyond the veils of tears and disbelief was the eruption of the calm and peace Dr. King marched for and was jailed for. Cities like New York, Los Angeles, and Washington, DC, felt the sting of the riots in their segregated communities. Baltimore was not immune to the dual pain of losing Dr. King and the riots that followed.

The irony was, months before Dr. King's death, he launched the Poor People's Campaign, working to help all races who were afflicted by the disease of poverty. And then here in my hometown, in Baltimore, as in other places, the community erupted in violence, hurting itself by inflicting its pain on the local Black economy the community relied so heavily on because of racial segregation. With our own hands, we further killed our dreams and hopes for a better community by destroying it as Dr. King tried to build it up . . . and more.

Bishop Vashti McKenzie can recall the corners of Pennsylvania Avenue and North Avenue, "Penn Central," very well, as it was near the house she grew up in on North Carey Street. Her memories are clear as to what she saw in 1965. As a young girl, she remembers seeing tears roll from her father's eyes as he was watching black-and-white TV news reports of peaceful Black protesters having hoses and dogs turned on them in Selma, Alabama. In 1968, immediately following the news of Dr. King's death, the young, inquisitive Vashti wanted to see what was going on in the streets outside her Baltimore City front door. Her parents said, "Don't go out!" She heeded their warnings. Yet McKenzie recalls, "Every place—Baltimore, Philadelphia, Los Angeles—had gone up, and it was just a matter of time that Baltimore would go up too!" Her personal level of anger was increasing. "I was incensed. You know, you're talking about a man of peace, who stood for peace, for nonviolence, all of a sudden was taken out violently, and I felt insulted as an American citizen that it would be troops in my neighborhood. I'd never seen anything like that before. I am talking huge trucks carrying the Army that is supposed to protect you. With guns on their backs."

As the trucks drove up and down the streets of her neighborhood, she questioned, "How could this be?" Baltimore was not alone. The National Guard was sent to cities like Washington, DC, and Los Angeles to help bring calm and restore order.

Broderick Johnson, President Barack Obama's cabinet secretary and head of the My Brother's Keeper initiative, is a Baltimore native. What he remembers is Pennsylvania Avenue in the 1970s as a street and an area "in transition." At that time, he worked in a men's store on Pennsylvania Avenue. He remembers the street was "still in transition," trying to recover after the riots of 1968. He says, "But over the next couple of years, it became a barren part of Baltimore, a dangerous part of Baltimore." He admits that part of Baltimore "started to die around the riots."

He was twelve when his family drove on that street in the aftermath of Dr. King's death. He remembers very vividly "riding up Pennsylvania Avenue" after church "that Sunday after King's death." There was "not a daytime curfew," so he saw firsthand what was going on in that area that was made up of poor people working to be in the middle class and some in the middle class working to sustain their lives and or do better economically. But how could they, when "the riots had taken a lot of Pennsylvania Avenue out?" And that was pretty much where Blacks were relegated to shop, as White establishments would not let them in.

He remembers hearing stories from family members about the vibrancy of some of the places in Baltimore's Black community prior to the 1968 riots. He cited Mondawmin Mall along with other mainstays once considered meccas for Black Baltimore. They lost their luster and began to tarnish after the riots. Yet these facilities continue, to this day, to house the memories of better years gone by and also the experiences of the new generations who utilize them.

But in the mid-70s, Johnson remembers, "It was still fairly vibrant with small clothing stores and the market. . . . Then over the next couple of decades it became a barren part of Baltimore and a very dangerous part of Baltimore."

Decades later, those memories came in like a flood for Johnson, when he traveled back to his hometown of Baltimore on April 27, 2015. His destination was the New Shiloh Baptist Church, a familiar facility. It is the place where his mother was a faithful member. But his intention this time was to represent the United States of America on behalf of the president, Barack Obama, at the funeral of twenty-five-year-old Freddie Gray: a man the Baltimore City state's attorney later found should not have been in police custody at all the day he died.

Johnson attended the funeral service, and it was emotionally tough. Just months earlier, his mother had been laid to rest in that same church where thousands came to say good-bye to Freddie Gray that Monday in April. Broderick's mother, as part of that church, was proud of her work as an usher. She was also a woman who did all she could to make sure her children had life chances, particularly in the real world of the streets of Baltimore.

During Gray's funeral, Johnson was reminded, constantly, that he could have been Freddie Gray or any other child or young adult facing an unfortunate situation. When Johnson's mother was alive, she told him the story of his second-grade experience at Public School #58 in the Park Circle community. That second-grade year was a major turning point for him. The teacher called his parents to offer up a status report that was not good. According to Johnson, the teacher said, "Your son is a knucklehead, and he is going to end up in reform school one day." Needless to say, his parents were not accepting the vision of that teacher's outcome for their child. A transition began. For many Blacks in Baltimore and other urban centers, to prevent the school-to-prison pipeline that has unfortunately become so commonplace, the saving grace is often private Catholic school. By third grade, the nuns were Johnson's teachers. And his path was no longer like the thousands who were trapped in the downward urban and minority spiral of drugs, gangs, joblessness, prison, and, in many cases, death.

At every milestone Johnson achieved, from graduations to passing the bar, his mother would remind him of how his life had changed in second grade. His parents ultimately paid Catholic school tuitions for all three of their children, to give them the best education they could. Johnson is the first to tell you, even from his high perch in the White House West Wing, "There but for the grace of God go I." The lesson was learned and was poignant enough that Johnson is now working to keep other kids in this nation from being a part of that vicious, destructive cycle.

Immediately following the Freddie Gray funeral, Johnson headed straight back to the White House. Once safely there, he began getting the reports that

Baltimore had erupted in those very spots he remembered growing up around. The mostly young crowd of angry rioters wanted immediate gratification in justice, not in the courtroom, but in the way they felt was real and right at the time: destruction of the area around them. Johnson, like so many others, watched the television news in horror. The kids clashed with police around the church where Freddie Gray's funeral had taken place. And then they moved to an even more common spot, Mondawmin Mall. The problem with Baltimore is "generational." As Johnson sees it, there is "still a lot of segregation in neighborhoods and professional career options."

No matter the heights you climb, the walls are still evident in the city that we call home. Johnson remembers wanting to come back home when he made something of himself. "The phenomenon in the '80s Baltimore was just not welcoming to a returning breed of Black leaders, people who had gone off to medical school and law school and wherever else and wanted to come back to Baltimore didn't develop . . . sort of a provincial thing."

To this day, Baltimore's social and professional communities are dictated by which high school and college you attended.

This spotlights the other side of the equation: what happens when you avoid that downward spiral and are still not accepted. It's a fact of life that some of us are blessed to leave in order to avoid that dangerous downward cycle in Baltimore and other areas. But the cycle does not always leave us. In fact, the cycle follows us no matter if we were in it or not. Even if we do successfully navigate a transition into a better life, there are still stark realities that easily draw us back to who they (mainstream society) believe we are and maybe where we originally started from.

Wes Moore says, life is colored differently for kids of pigment versus White children. He says, "Kids of color versus kids who are not of color do not get the same runway, as is the same scenario for kids who come up in lower income communities than for kids who don't."

Author and chief executive officer of BridgeEdU, Moore remembers being a kid who did not like to read. His mother would trick him into reading by quizzing him on the sports magazines she would purchase to spark his interest in the written word. That spurred his love of reading and writing while many of his contemporaries were not as fortunate. His mother, who still resides in Baltimore, was his saving grace. For him and many other Blacks, it is about walking the fine dividing line between two polar opposite worlds.

There are distinct differences in Moore's childhood and his acclaimed life today. Vividly, he remembers, "I was never a bad kid. 'Cause, actually, I don't think so many of our kids are bad kids. I really was a kid truly trying to find a level of acceptance. And I was willing to do what it took to find acceptance. And unfortunately I was trying to find acceptance from people . . . I was repeatedly finding a way to hurt people that actually loved me, so I could impress people that did not. That was just my M.O. I wanted so much to be accepted. I wanted so much to be taken in, that I was yearning to be taken in by bullies who did not have my best interest at heart."

The lifestyle Moore grew up in, and the one he lives in now, with his family, as an adult are very different. An example of the reality of that was his move back to Baltimore after he had left and made a name for himself as author, motivational speaker, and much more. Moore says, "First it was amazing how many of my friends, who when I told them we were moving back to Baltimore, because we were living in New York, I could sum up their reaction in one word. That word was 'Why?' People didn't understand why I was moving back from New York to move back home."

He moved from New York back to Baltimore in 2013. Tongues were wagging. It caused people to question his motives. They wondered what was happening. His friends were asking, "Is everything okay? Is your mom okay?" The answer was yes!

Moore told them, "Everything is fine." Like Broderick Johnson, he just yearned for the city he grew up in. He did not have to be there but chose to come back. But, unlike Johnson, Moore did come back home. But the irony was, when his wife went house searching, she found a home in the prestigious community of Guilford, in the area down the road from Johns Hopkins University. The name of the community took Moore back to his childhood and the haunts of his painful past.

Moore remembers, "As soon as she [his wife] said 'Guilford,' my understanding of it as a child came up, and Guilford was this area where literally the past twenty-five years Blacks weren't even allowed to buy properties in Guilford. Blacks and Jews were not allowed in Guilford. It was on the deeds."

The Baltimore Wes Moore remembers from decades ago was a city where "there were certain neighborhoods in Baltimore you just don't go for safety reasons and safety purposes. And not safety purposes of danger. But for safety purposes of, 'I don't want the cops stopping you.' And 'I don't want people calling the cops when they see you walking through the neighborhood because you don't belong there.'"

All this as his wife is not from Baltimore and not hip to the racist history of the town. "It was something, this reconciling . . . to exist in two worlds, a place that you kind of romanticize about this idea of quote unquote going home but understanding that there is a clear and a distinct and, quite honestly, a heartbreaking reality for a lot of people about what Baltimore is and what Baltimore means and about a Baltimore we all hope to live in. I am very fortunate now that I feel like there is nothing in Baltimore that surprises me on either side. So I am able to see things from so many different perspectives. At the same time it is a very clear reminder of just how separate these worlds are."

For others it is about the unmistakable reality of what happens by being Black, even when you live a life of privilege and affluence and come from the "right" family.

Valerie Jarrett grew up in Chicago in the 1960s where both of her parents illuminated their personal stories of racism to give her context and to show how and when things began to change. Both her parents attended segregated schools, her mother in Chicago and her father in Washington, DC. They discussed racially restrictive covenants that prohibited the purchase, lease, or occupation of a piece of property by a particular group of people, usually African Americans, even if the owner desired this transaction.

Jarrett's mom gave her stories about traveling to the South, to states like North Carolina and to cities like Tuskegee, Alabama, when she was a child. She told her daughter how she would have to stay in people's homes while traveling to their destination because Black people could not stay in hotels. The Civil Rights Act of 1964 prohibited discrimination based on race, color, religion, sex, or national origin in public places and provided for the integration of schools and other public facilities and made employment discrimination illegal.

As Jarrett grew up in affluence, the dark reality of the African American community hit her street. Valerie recalls, "I remember seeing my mother jump out of our car because two of our neighbors were pulled over by the police. And I can remember going, 'Why are you getting out of the car?' And she said, 'I want to make sure those boys are okay.'"

Jarrett was about ten or eleven years old at the time and the boys were about fourteen and sixteen years old. They all lived on the same block. A parent of one of the boys was an English professor at the University of Chicago, and the other boy's parents were both psychiatrists. The boys were walking down the block without ID cards. In the 1960s that was their crime and almost similar to what happens today. Jarrett recalls being both terrified and proud of her mother's actions. She recalls her mother saying, "I had to look out for those boys because I didn't know what would happen." It was a "profound experience" that made her afraid of the police for a long time.

But years later, when Jarrett was sixteen, she took driver's ed training about two miles from her home. After the class, as she was coming home from the session, she stood at the bus stop, and she remembers, "The skies opened up and it started pouring down rain," and a police car pulled over. A White policeman told her, "Get in the car." Jarrett remembers, "I thought I was a goner." She was "terrified." She immediately remembered the incident with the two boys on her block. Jarrett complied with what the officer ordered. She got in the car thinking she would go to the police station and never be seen again. But it was the polar opposite. They took her home, pulled up in her driveway, and told her, "Next time wear a raincoat. And be careful."

"It was interesting, as that was not what I had expected," according to Jarrett. She went on to say, "It made me realize I should not judge all police by that incident." Jarrett is thankful, saying, "It was good experience to see both." When it comes to matters of race, Jarrett says, "Over the last couple of years in particular, there has now been a spotlight. The fact is that we still have extraordinary inequity in this country. And we still have discrimination and racism. That shouldn't come as any surprise! None of us should be under any illusion that just by electing an African American president that generations of the legacy of racism was going to evaporate overnight."

★ ★ ★

No words rang truer on February 23, 2016. I can only examine the city in which I grew up to use as an example. My beloved Baltimore is the backdrop for this chapter. I see a great city, diverse in every way. But what you see through that camera lens or on a train ride into the most blighted areas of the city is just a small, straw-hole glimpse of the whole story. As to who we are as a people, that is something totally different. There is wealth, there is poverty; there is hurt, but there is also hope. When you think of Baltimore and the surrounding area, no matter who you are, look at it as a city of survival. Everyone, no matter what station in life, is trying to survive and make things happen to better their economic situation.

For me, this double-life matter shook my core, in a life or death drama that played out on the public stage. February 22, 2016, I was not immune to the ugliness of the streets of my beloved city of Baltimore as I sat 150 feet from the seat of power, the Oval Office. I was at the White House briefing, where Press Secretary Josh Earnest was delivering his daily update. I had received several phone calls from my aunt. Where I was located, I couldn't answer the phone right away. I knew something was wrong because she kept calling me. I waited for the hour-plus briefing to end. It was longer that day because several governors addressed the crowd about their meeting with the president. Virginia Governor Terry McAuliffe was one of them, and I even got a chance to ask a question of him.

But once the briefing ended, I called my aunt, who ultimately told me, while I was still sitting in the Briefing Room with people around me, that both my uncle and another aunt (his sister) had been shot. My Uncle Gill had been wounded in the leg, and my Aunt Martha had been shot in the leg as well. Apparently, she had also been grazed by another bullet. I couldn't believe it, and it took me more than an hour to calm down. After I was able to take in what had happened, I thought about it during the hour-long drive back to Baltimore, more than fifty miles away. I was in shock as I realized this was the first shooting that had ever happened in my family. This was my eighty-two-year-old uncle and godfather and his ninety-two-year-old sister. I realized that no one is immune, even as I work in this White House world, but I'm still pulled back to the ugly dynamics of my community at a moment's notice no matter where I am. Living in two worlds is a very real dynamic for many people. I call it the "dual world syndrome."

My Uncle Gill is my second father! When I was a baby, he and his wife, my Aunt Pearl, went before the church and acknowledged they would take care of me in the event anything happened to my parents. They became my godparents that day! My mother used to live with my aunt, her blood sister, and my aunt's husband, Uncle Gill, when she first moved to Baltimore. Uncle Gill worked with my dad at the Mass Transit Administration for a stint. It was my Uncle Gill who introduced my parents.

Uncle Gill was the one who helped me obtain my driver's license after I failed the driving portion of the test numerous times. He took me out on the streets of Baltimore over and over again and showed me how to maneuver some of the most complicated turns and how to park in the city. My Uncle Gill, as we affectionately call him, is one of the gentlest souls you will ever find. He enjoys children immensely, loving to make them smile and laugh. He always engages every baby and kid in the family. He sang in his AME Church choir in inner-city Baltimore. He loves the outdoors, from fishing to hunting. As an outdoorsman, he may have picked up this love from his rural upbringing in South Carolina. As a child, I remember the common sight of fresh fish packed in ice in a large cooler in the kitchen of their Northeast Baltimore home, literally blocks from my house at the time. For some reason, seeing the fish made me want to go on the water with him to get the biggest catch. I would beg Uncle Gill to take me fishing, and he would jokingly tell me, "It is bad luck to take a woman fishing."

Well, I think I fell in love with the peace and tranquility of fishing through him. I would see his catch from his many fishing trips and watch my Aunt Pearl scale and clean the fish with its clear, white protective covering, its scales, popping everywhere. Aunt Pearl would tell me that Uncle Gill would be on the boat before sunrise for his catch, and boy did he bring home lots! That was the best-tasting fresh fish ever! I believe I ultimately began fishing in my twenties, in Chattanooga, and then picked it back up in my late thirties because he made it look exciting.

And then there was hunting. I remember numerous times my Aunt Pearl would tell me there was venison in the fridge. I never ate it, but they did. They even consumed it when it was given as a gift from friends who would go hunting for deer. I don't know and I never asked if Uncle Gill owned a gun, but I knew he enjoyed game hunting.

Fast-forwarding to 2016, this shooting still is unbelievable for my family, as we had never been touched like this before. Make no mistake, I am not saying this should not have or could not have happened to us. I have always understood a bullet has no name on it, but I am still shaking my head in disbelief that, of all people, my Uncle Gill was shot. He is literally the man who would give you anything if you needed it or asked. He is a man who would, without batting an eye, mentor a child or take a family member to a drug rehab center, because that's just who he is. He is also the man who enlisted his wife to help care for his elderly sister who lives in West Baltimore. It was nothing for either of them to go to her house a couple of times a week and take her to the Asian grocery store in the county, to the bank, or anywhere she needed to go.

When the shooting happened at Walbrook Junction, at one o'clock in the afternoon, people were moving about that community as they do every day. It's a neighborhood more than familiar to my uncle, as he has lived there for over forty-one years. They moved there from a home just blocks away after the birth of my cousin, their daughter. The shooting happened in broad daylight and caught us all off guard, as no one saw it coming. The saving grace of this horrid event is that it was caught on tape. The suspect was deemed by the Baltimore City Police Department as "Public Enemy Number One" because he did the unthinkable. He unintentionally shot two elderly people. From what I understand, one of the worst things you can do is harm the elderly, children, and babies! Well, those two people were an elderly brother and sister, my uncle by marriage, Hogan McGill, and his sister, Martha Gilliard.

The manhunt was on! The initial news reports were very wrong. They were saying my uncle and his sister were walking to the bus stop. I went on Twitter saying that was incorrect. My Uncle Gill was taking Aunt Martha to run errands, as he has in the past. This time they were in the area and were walking to a carry-out for a sandwich, and then my uncle said he heard "Bam, bam, bam!" He said people went running and screaming. He was standing the entire time, and then he was shot in the leg, and Aunt Martha went down after also being shot in the leg, and then a bullet grazed her head.

I was late, but I finally made it to the family waiting area of the hospital. I saw a lot of my family there, including my aunt and uncle's daughter, with her son and husband. I asked if I could go in and see them, and she gave the okay. I did. I was so nervous! It had taken me more than an hour to get myself together at the White House before I took that long ride home to see the aftermath of this careless and senseless crime.

All I remember is getting off the elevator and not knowing exactly where to go. I turned right and then walked down a short hall and into the shock-trauma unit. I was walking down this long hall and realized my uncle was right there in my line of sight. Police were dotted all around the unit as a precaution. This is common police procedure when a shooting happens. When I got to his room and I approached his hospital gurney bed, I said, "Now you know you didn't need to do this to get my attention." He smiled at me. But as he lay in that very vulnerable position I realized I had never in my forty-eight years seen him in, I could not hold back telling him how God was in this. The only other time I saw my uncle tear up is when I told him my mother was dying. At that moment, a flood of water welled up in his eyes. He held back the flow by lifting his head toward the ceiling.

I know it could have easily gone the other way. We could have, that day, been planning one or even two funerals. I am not saying we should be immune to this. My heart breaks to hear this is happening in so many communities, and now, so close, in my family.

I talked with Uncle Gill and Aunt Pearl for a while, and then I moved down to the other unit, where Aunt Martha was alone. She was in a shock-trauma room down the hall and to the left. When I saw her, she was confused. She did not remember me, but she trusted me. She also didn't remember my children, who frequented her home with my Aunt Pearl. She trusted me to help her. Aunt Martha was agitated and was complaining of being cold. She wanted her clothes, but those clothes had been cut off her so emergency personnel could find out if she had been shot anywhere else.

When the officer who was on post at her room told her, "The clothes were evidence," Aunt Martha became more distraught. She cried a bit, and then began asking, "Where is my baby brother?" I kept telling her Uncle Gill was here and down the hall. But she wouldn't calm down. My words were not enough. She needed to put her eyes on her brother. As she remained very agitated, I asked the doctor if my cousin could come up, as two people were allowed in each room. It was not good. My cousin came and calmed her, but she was still very anxious. She never complained about the leg that had a bullet wound, or her head where you could see the large bloody area where the bullet had grazed her. During this incident, Aunt Martha had fallen to the ground, was scraped, and broke her glasses when she was shot.

But at a point, she was discharged and was wheeled to my Uncle Gill's room. She was relieved and not as upset. I was blessed that night to take both of them to their homes. During the ride back from the hospital in my mini-van, Aunt Martha kept saying, "In all my life I haven't had anything like this happen to me." My uncle responded, saying, "It happened and we have to thank and pray to God!"

During the weeks of healing, Uncle Gill said he wanted the suspect caught, saying "he needed to get help." The police apparently had him cornered and he eventually turned himself in. The suspect, whose name I won't use, gave himself up to police in Fayetteville, North Carolina. They penned him in. He could not go home again. The police had been in conversation with his wife, who said he had told her he was shooting at someone who shot at him first. And there it was, the admission of guilt!

Ironically, Baltimore City State's Attorney Marilyn Mosby did visit the elderly brother and sister who were shot. She made it to the hospital bedside of both of my relatives, not knowing they were my family members. Meanwhile, the young, groundbreaking, African American city attorney is a native of Boston, unfortunately another city that has its own race issues. She recognizes the cities are comparable in their populations, but for Baltimore and matters of race, she feels more "optimistic." The question is why? Mosby offers, "When I came here [Baltimore] there was a Black woman who was mayor, there was a Black woman state's attorney. There was a Black comptroller, there was a Black president of the City Council. . . . When you look at every urban city there is always segregation. But when you look at Baltimore there is that optimism . . . you can dream and you can achieve it, especially as an African American woman."

The backstory for Mosby is that she and her mother were the first Black kids in their respective schools' integration efforts on busing in the Boston area school district. Her mother went through the same metro program in the 1970s as she did. The Mosbys were always vocal about race relations, and race has always been an issue. With a heart to help, the Mosby family, including her two children, reside in what was once considered one of the worst communities in Baltimore City, in an effort to change the dynamic and offer assistance. Mosby says that other than occasional people being upset with her decisions, she has no problems living in her predominantly Black and economically challenged neighborhood.

Mosby first balked at her husband's vision of living in the Whitelock area of the city, emphasizing, "Are you crazy? This is where you want to raise our family?" She looked at the "open-air drug market and the trash on the street, the number of vacant houses on the street." Her husband thought it was about having the vision and foresight for their dream house, so that they could be examples for this community. She trusted him and says twelve years later there are no vacant homes on the street, no open-air drug markets, and very little trash. A complex called "murder mall" near their home was also shut down. She says that was "one of the best decisions in my life," offering the possibilities of the future. "It was about having that vision and foresight, and being the example. That is a microcosm for the potential of Baltimore City."

• 8 •

Assimilation

$\mathcal{M}$y mind screams "identity" for the word, *assimilation*. But it also begs the question, assimilation without the loss of identity or the strengthening of who you are? Or is it really about a melding of people?

Actress Erika Alexander, who has appeared as Maxine in the TV show *Living Single*, Cousin Pam on *The Cosby Show*, and is currently on the shows *Bosch*, *Queen Sugar*, and *Beyond*, was asked her first thoughts about the word *assimilation*. What came to her mind? "Annihilation. Dilution. To fit into. Or, more optimistically and in the spirit of a modern-day slang, a new-age, brain-drained mashup! Assimilation is the filtered absence of what originally makes you, you. You become 'curated.'"

For this book and specifically this chapter, I asked a simple question about the initial thoughts on the word *assimilation*. In her Baltimore, Maryland, office, I asked Baltimore City State's Attorney Marilyn Mosby her thoughts. This word was perfectly suited for her, as she walks in boldness, bucking the system and the seemingly status quo agenda. So when I asked the celebrated and yet reviled African American woman the question, what came to her mind was "conformity." When asked if she is a conformist, she said, "Nope!"

Conformity is one definite way to look at this complex issue. In recent years, we have heard the conversations about assimilation ever so loudly in Washington as government leaders continue to wrestle with immigration issues. For example, people want those who speak other languages to learn English when they come to this country.

But when I personally think of the word, I think of my mother and her conversations about the historic doll test. For better or worse, it is a very real issue. My mother reminded me constantly as a child of the Black doll test. The doll test was conducted about fourteen years prior to *Brown vs. Board of*

Education in order to scientifically assess the self-esteem of Black children. The NAACP Legal Defense Fund website, www.naacpldf.org/brown-at-60-the-doll-test, contends that

> In the 1940s, psychologists Kenneth and Mamie Clark designed and conducted a series of experiments known colloquially as "the doll tests" to study the psychological effects of segregation on African-American children.
>
> Drs. Clark used four dolls, identical except for color, to test children's racial perceptions. Their subjects, children between the ages of three to seven, were asked to identify both the race of the dolls and which color doll they prefer. A majority of the children preferred the white doll and assigned positive characteristics to it. The Clarks concluded that "prejudice, discrimination, and segregation" created a feeling of inferiority among African-American children and damaged their self-esteem.
>
> The doll test was only one part of Dr. Clark's testimony in *Brown*—it did not constitute the largest portion of his analysis and expert report. His conclusions during his testimony were based on a comprehensive analysis of the most cutting-edge psychology scholarship of the period.

In the 1940s, the study was laser focused on the self-esteem of Black children. According to Dr. Clark, one of the results from his testing of a child in Arkansas spoke volumes. A Black child was asked which doll was most like him. The child answered by pointing at a Black doll. The doctor said the child was smiling when he gave his answer and then said, "That's a *nigger*. I am a *nigger*." Needless to say, Dr. Clark found the answer "disturbing."

Judge Mablean Ephriam says, "They started making a few Black dolls when my daughter was born. I didn't buy White dolls." She was adamant in her feelings to her daughter, saying, "No, no, no, you are going to play with dolls that look like you. You are not going to play with dolls that look like other people. You are going to play with dolls that look like you. You are going to love you." She went further, telling her daughter, dolls of other races in your possession "are designed for you to hate *you*." She said all the symbols of beauty are "long 'white' hair. No, no, no! You are just as beautiful!"

The issue of self-esteem is very real in the Black community to this day. It takes strength for this admission, even for the strongest of persons. Maryland Congressman Elijah Cummings says he battles daily with low self-esteem issues. Cummings is a fierce fighter for truth and justice. It almost sounds like an advertisement for a superhero, but it is true for this native of Baltimore. Looking back over his life, Cummings acknowledges, there but for the grace of God, his life story should have been different. He says he was labeled as a special education kid, but then became a lawyer and is now the bulldog for the Democratic Party, leading the way in the powerful Oversight and Government Reform Committee in the House of Representatives. Cummings says,

"We've got self-esteem problems, a lot of us. It comes from the way we were treated as children."

The conversation hits closer to home when Cummings reveals that the doll test results were used in *Brown vs. Board of Education*, which consisted of five different cases, and some of his relatives were represented in that historic moment, and also in another case against the education system. But he admits, "We truly underestimate the lack of self-esteem in our community." He floored me with this admission: "All my life I battle with self-esteem. All my life!" During the interview, I instantly responded, "Are you kidding me?" To me he is a man who exudes confidence and strength and would go toe to toe with the best of them. He is someone whom I view as a protector of his friends and family, someone you would not cross. But he has a battle like many of us. His self-esteem doubts are rooted in his early years as a child in Baltimore when he was one of many children who were part of efforts to integrate White swimming pools in Baltimore City. His mother was right there walking her children to the pool as White people taunted and jeered them. He also remembers the inequity of having to wait in long lines for shoes and clothes, as Black people could not shop where the White people did. He said, "Oh yeah! I fight that sucka [low self-esteem]! I have to fight it! Think about what I said. You go to a school as a little kid, in like a nine- or ten-room school, and then you see the White people go into a big school. Kids always remember. They don't process information like adults. We are intellectual. Kids are emotional. I have often said it is not the deed. It is the memory. In other words you remember how you were treated. People are haunted by memories. Memories are a bugga bear. There are people so haunted by memories today that they can't even move. It is almost impossible for them to accomplish anything. They remember something that happened when they were a little kid. . . . It comes from the way we were treated as children."

Interestingly enough, growing up in the 1970s, my bedroom was filled with stuffed animals, a Raggedy Ann doll, and a Black baby doll I called Vicky. She was beautiful with eyelids that would open and shut. Her eyes glistened as if they were made of crystals of amber. She was a beautiful darker hue with this brownish-red straight hair in a bob hairstyle. She wore knitted white baby booties with flower appliqués and a pretty pink and white checked baby doll dress with matching bloomers. I was not one of those girls who always played with dolls, but I loved Vicky. As a kid, I imagined that my child someday would look like Vicky.

My mother reinforced my identity as an aspiring young woman who could grow up to work and live in multicultural places, not all Black and not all White but more inclusive than what she had seen in her life. I attended grade school and high school in predominantly White settings with very few Black people.

Things were changing, as my mother wanted me to live and work differently than she did, in a society she had not really seen before.

My mother worked hard to reinforce the identities of both her children. Ironically, I am finding myself engaging in similar conversations with my own daughters. This time their world has opened wider for them, larger than mine and my mother's before me, and of course, her mother's. Today we live in a mixed community, and my girls attend a predominantly White, affluent school. But issues of identity are important still. I have had to talk about the dolls with both my girls, as they have chosen to have both Black and White dolls in their rooms. When questioned about why have a White doll, they said they have White friends, and why not have a White doll? I could not say anything, but when I asked "What doll do you identify with?" they picked the doll that looked like them.

Like many families, we were smitten by that certain expensive doll that has characters from slavery through different periods in history. Each year, the company chooses a doll to highlight. My older daughter, Ryan, wanted "Lanie," a White doll that reminded her of her best friend at the time. She also has a "Ryan" doll, a doll that looks like her. And my baby, Grace, wanted the White doll that carried her name. That was her reasoning for the doll. But we were a year too late for that doll, so she ecstatically settled on the doll that looked like her. She has not parted with that doll since we purchased it. Meanwhile, this conversation about assimilation reminded me that I never discussed the doll test with them. That has since changed.

Successful African American woman Loni Love recalls she was a latchkey kid growing up. She was a child who understood her mom had to work, and she cared for herself after school by walking home and doing homework and watching TV until her mother returned home from work. I understand that concept, as it mirrors my childhood. She grew up in an all-Black housing project in Detroit and never had a conversation with her mother about race. She reflected, thinking about that only when I asked her questions for this book.

She grew up around Blacks and no other racial community, saying, "The way I grew up, it has affected the way I treat people. There was never anything planted in my mind saying, 'Oh, you know, White people act this way and Black people act this way.'" But she is keenly aware of how who we are plays into perceptions and realities for other cultures when it comes to people finding their identity culturally and independently. "When it comes to assimilation, there is a difference to me in cultural appropriation and cultural assimilation. Cultural assimilation is what I had to do when I was an engineer. I couldn't work as an engineer and have an Afro. I wouldn't have gotten the job if I had, you know, locks or braids at the time. That was in the late 1990s, early 2000s. If you wanted a job, to be considered professional you had to have straight hair or your hair in a nice neat bun. But there was no such thing as having an Afro or things like that. So I actually assimilated because I needed to make a living. And also, you have to dress a certain way. And they call it business attire, but it is still to me a European type of attire. And that's assimilation. And that's something I had to do. And as a young girl, when you are put under that type of assimilation, it really makes you open up your mind to decide, 'Okay, what is it that I want to do with my life? Do I want to walk around and have my hair straight, wear this suit and these heels that hurt, or is there another type of life for me?' And that is part of what made me say I don't want to be part of corporate America. I have to find something in life that I can do."

Today, either when she is acting, hosting a television talk show, or doing her stand-up comedy routine, Loni rocks her braids unapologetically and with great pride.

When William Jefferson Clinton was the president, he met with genetic scientists, who gave him a nugget he constantly referenced. Clinton reiterated over and over again about the human genome and that we are all 99.9 percent the same. Our chemical makeup is the same, from one person to the next. But that fact never translated to society in ways to make a difference in bridging the ugly racial divide that still haunts this nation. Despite our genetic similarities, we are all uniquely made. Yet the unwritten rule is that we must conform to popular standards and social norms. But when we work to be our best selves and live our best lives, where does our uniqueness and difference fit in as we assimilate with the mainstream?

When looking for ways to move forward in dealing with the sensitive matters of race, the influence of wisdom and firsthand experience of the past is a reference point. Much of the current divisive dialogue and hate-filled actions are nothing new, but are a cyclical dynamic of the hypersensitivity that perpetually surrounds matters of race in this nation. History supports the fact that racial tensions began with the colonization of this country. But as we fight for our individual and collective identities, we are also encouraged to assimilate, to become uniform with others.

Activist and entertainer Harry Belafonte says, "Assimilation, the first thought that comes to mind when I think of assimilation is I think about the need for us to be more trusting, more embracing, more committed to the beauty of diversity rather than look at diversity as a threat, as something to compete with, as something to be contained and relegated in a lesser place in our social engagement. We should look upon these things as opportunity. As I look at the assimilation, integration, and all the things we aspire to, or I aspire to, in all my life working with Dr. King, Nelson Mandela, Eleanor Roosevelt, and all the great figures of our time who I was privileged to be in the service of. I also looked upon diversity as an instrument of opportunity."

Author Wes Moore was asked what comes to mind when he thinks of the word *assimilation*. "I almost feel like the word I would use more would be 'adapt.' I think I have adapted well. I don't have a goal of transforming to a point that I become unrecognizable. Either by the way I become unrecognizable or even in my own heart or my own mind that I no longer become unrecognizable in my own mind. . . . I think exposure has helped me to adapt. Exposure has helped me have a different set of goals and aspirations, but I really hope I never 'assimilate.' If I never assimilate, I will never lose that sense of compassion about what we see now."

When asked what she thought of the word *assimilation*, Iyanla Vanzant said during the phone interview, "I think it is dangerous." She remembers how her spiritual life clashed with her mainstream work life in her budding legal career. She had achieved something very special. She passed her bar exam and purchased a shingle; she was a practicing attorney with some cases going before a judge. But at that same time she was true to herself and her faith. She became a "newly initiated Yoruba priestess," her calling in the ministry. As a requirement for her first-year "initiation process" as a priestess, she "had to wear white for a year." The attire was all white with no splash of color or any variations to the requirement. "So I had suits, white dresses, white shoes, white coat, white everything." This even applied to her professional life. Vanzant did not waver in her conviction.

She found professional white attire. But there was a clash. The clash was with a judge who could not understand why she was always adorned in white when she came into his courtroom. She remembers laughingly, like it was yesterday, "The judge says to me, literally from the bench, asked me why I had on white." Her answer: "for religious purposes." The judge inquired about the religion, and she informed him and the others in the courtroom who could hear, that she was "a Yoruba priestess." Yoruba is a Southwestern Nigerian religion. The judge retorted that he never heard of that. That was the end of that round of questioning. But after coming into his courtroom a few times later in her all-white attire, he said to young attorney Vanzant, "When you come into my courtroom, I want you dressed appropriately or properly!" Vanzant did not remember her exact words, but she said to the judge, "I am dressed appropriately." The judge firmly said, "No, you should have on a black or brown or blue or gray clothing." Vanzant told the judge she did not own those items, and he followed up, telling her she should own one. The judge told her, "If you come into my courtroom again dressed like that, I am going to hold you in contempt."

Vanzant says, "People are more comfortable with you when you look like they need you to look in order for them to be comfortable." It was baffling to Vanzant, as she was walking in her truth. "Now I can't imagine why white clothes would disturb somebody." The drama continued when she went back into the same courtroom. The judge sternly reminded her, "Didn't I tell you if you came into my courtroom again dressed improperly, that I would have you cited for contempt?" Vanzant, standing firm in her belief, said, "Here's the check for the fine." After that exchange, she worked to get a reasonable answer as to why he was upset with her professional yet white attire, asking, "What I'd really like to know is what disturbs you about my attire? My knees are covered, my shoulders are covered, my décolletage is covered; I mean I am covered. I would just like to understand." Not only was her outfit not politically correct in the judge's eyes, but she also stood out wearing white in the month of December. She clearly stood out!

Looking back, she is reminded of similar fights for African American attorneys, both male and female, with dreadlocks and braids in the courtroom. There were lawsuits. Yet returning to her issue, Iyanla said, "I will take off my white when the Jews take off their yarmulke." She affirms they wear yarmulkes in the courtroom. She contends, "We cannot as people allow someone to strip us of our sense of self. I just think that is dangerous when we assimilate to the point where you show up in a way that just makes other people comfortable and has no meaning or bearing on the truth of who you are. I just think it is a problem."

Actress Erika Alexander offers a similar thought regarding the melding of who you are with the mainstream world. She says, "The 'new' you becomes an amalgamation of your adopted tribe. Your looks, personality, and culture are encouraged to conform and fit into the host culture's specific, fixed, crowd-tested point of view. The result is a world where outsiders become insiders by absorbing the dominant culture's habits, style, and traditions. You are deemed successful if you are able to absorb then reconstruct yourself, then skillfully reflect a predigested, regurgitated version of the preapproved, road-tested, ideal version of the mob."

One major question is, should people of color assimilate with the mainstream? Alexander is very strong in her thoughts about this, saying, "This may be controversial, but I believe that if 'the mainstream' is hostile or aggressive toward outsiders, it may be a 'strategic move' of survival to assimilate. Personally, I don't believe in race-based assimilation, but I do believe in survival. In other words, 'win the day.' What to some may look like ceding ground may, in hindsight, be cloaking oneself in order to avoid detection. Black people are pragmatists by necessity, and we unfairly face invisible barriers everywhere, so it's reasonable for us to try to take the road of least resistance. Assimilation is one of them, but usually to no avail. Our mainstream 'costume' may eventually fit, but from the dominant, White point of view, our Blackness still stains our pressed, bleached, white collars. They will find us out.

"Fortunately, time is not static; neither are traditions, culture, or mind-sets. The African American spirit is so strong, so creative, so dominant, that it has become the 'marker.' It is the preferred flavor that the world desires to emulate. Imagine that, originally owned and oppressed, we were bred to be dominated and to recede into the shadows. But instead the stellar talents and accomplishments of our people infected the mind-sets of the people who bred us, so much so, we own them. Hearts and minds."

Another actress, Rae Dawn Chong, contends she never had the talk with her mom about race. In her e-mail response, she wrote, "Nothing. I grew up in Canada and maybe as a reflective survival response race was never brought up by my mother. Plus everyone we saw in Vancouver in the 1960s was a relation. Cousin this or auntie that. So in my perception we were all family, those of us of brown skin. Which is tragic because as young girls we were ill-equipped for the United States, the home of bigotry. I kid. I know there is bigotry in Canada and we did experience it, only it was milder and less abrasive. In fact the biggest experience of racism came from my uncle and cousins. They were the first to let me and my sister know Black was less than. I mean, we both rejected this and fought it our entire lives. Still, within my family we were reminded of our color. Funny, because I always felt my sister and I were extra special in a positive way so we thought 'they' were just jealous. LOL we were so adorable. In defense of our mom, there wasn't a need to explain. It just never was a 'thing' even if it was. We coped and were educated about the struggle decades later in the USA."

Chong said, "The conversation has never happened. We were thrust on our own into the world of film and TV, where it was very prevalent, as I wasn't allowed to read for things or I lost gigs because of my color. It was the 1970s when I started to work. In fact my friend's mom reminded me that after years of working, she mentioned to me that every part I had gotten was token. She was right and she was a jealous bitch too, but she was right. It scared me, her comment, but looking back now, I know she was right and she was being mean because her daughter never amounted to much although we were contemporaries, her daughter and I. My vulnerability against the racism that I experienced socially and professionally was something I was not warned about or prepared for. I suffered greatly. I was devastated that it was there and stubbornly ignored it. To my detriment, because decades later I was called out for ignoring my race. You see I had to keep working, being cast as a character versus 'Blackting' or as a 'Blacktor' which is still prevalent and popular. I commend the people who cast me for character versus as the token spook. But then the very thing that carries you (me) can be used against you and so we almost never win. Being from Canada there is this unspoken thing where race isn't brought up, at least in my immediate family it wasn't a thing."

Unfortunately, Judge Mablean Ephriam contends, "Integration in my opinion has had a negative impact. Because once we began to assimilate into the world where distinctions were not made, we lost our identities. We assimilated so we could lose our identities. . . . Some of us don't even want to identify as Black, African American . . . God made all these different races, all these different creeds, all these different looks, and hair and the texture. He did it for a reason. He did not want for us all to look the same. He did not want a monochromatic society . . . We have lost our own sense of identity and who we are and our own values where we no longer value ourselves and value our work."

One of the most surprising responses to my question about "What are your first thoughts on the word *assimilation?*" was from Maryland 7th District Congressman Elijah Cummings, who said what first comes to mind with the word *assimilation* is "integration." He used the example of his mother at his home for a family dinner at Christmas, December 2015. Cummings remembers, "We have a real big family." It was a mixed-race gathering of about fifty people.

He noticed his mother was surveying the room with some emotion. Cummings asked his ninety-year-old mother, "Why are you looking like that?" Cummings recalls, she whispered in his ear, "I never thought as a little girl, I would have White people in my family!" Cummings laughingly says, "It was a lot of them too!" It was a poignant moment for his mother. He added, "This was a woman who saw prejudice to the nth degree!" She witnessed the evolution, over her nine decades, of deep racism. Ultimately, White people were coming to her saying, "Hi, Momma!" Cummings said this family called her "Momma" out of respect.

· 9 ·

Work-Life Balance

$\mathcal{A}$s mothers, our influence and our examples are the most powerful. If I am honest with myself, I am my mother. She did it all! She worked long hours on a job and loved every minute of it. As she fulfilled her purpose, she also made sure her family was taken care of, be it cooking, taking clothes to the cleaners, taking children to the doctors, housework, or making breakfast, lunch, and dinner. Her family, particularly my dad, who had a special diet, was always taken care of. All this, as she worked in a very demanding job on a college campus, helping young, budding professionals expand their experiences during their college years.

Like my mother, I carry around bags of work with me. My mother would take work with her no matter where she was in an effort to find time to finish papers, bills, or her homework, as she was trying to obtain her master's degree just before she died. I find myself doing the same thing. She was my shining example. A real superwoman! Even though she was married, my mother did the lion's share of the work. She was the backbone of our home. The roles were clear, whether we call it "old school" or just the way it worked for them. My dad and mom both brought home the bacon; however, my mom was the emotional and physical anchor and everything else in our home. I don't know how she did it. Because at the same time, she was rising up the ranks at her job, and she obtained a college degree while I was in high school.

She is still known in the community as an exceptional woman, more than nine years after her death. Her presence in the community, as well as in our homes and hearts, is sorely missed. She showered both my brother and me with so much love! She was a diligent and remarkable worker, revered on her job by all whose hearts she touched and worked with. She was involved in social organizations and active in her church. Mary Vivian Gowans Ryan

thrived in every facet of her life. She literally glowed in her versatility, especially when she worked to help her children navigate the waters of youth. In
her gentle and kind ways, she shielded my brother and me from the ugliness
of people and bad intentions from family, friends, or people on the street.
Likewise, she was there when there was discord in the family. In many ways
we, as people, reflect our upbringing and parenting, whether biological or
otherwise. Some days I see my reflection in my mother, with her work ethic,
nurturing of children, and networking in business.

But unlike my mother, who was married "until death do us part," I am
now the sole breadwinner in my household. Reverend Iyanla Vanzant, author
and spiritual life coach, puts it best: "What you have to do and how you have
to do it, all the emphasis is on making the money and providing for the kids."
I am part of that unplugged sorority of single mothers who do their best at
raising their children, working to make it all come together for the greater
good of the family.

So when I look at my life, I see a reflection that is my mother. She was
powerfully remarkable. There are days that are overwhelming, and I feel as if
I can hardly tread water. But there are also days when it all comes together.
Some days I am fortunate that I strike the chord where the kids are fed,
homework is done, and some of my writing and reporting is finished. My
extended family is okay, and after the 100 miles I burn up driving to and from
Washington, DC, for work, the car is still running well!

I'm able to admit, without hesitation, that I am trying to make it all
work. However, *trying* is the operative word. Yes, I know the word *trying* has
an automatic assumption of possible defeat. But it's true, it does not always
come together. I am a divorced mother, working in an entirely different city
from where I live, with children in an expensive private school I work very
hard to afford. For the most part, there is a constant teetering effort between
it working and my trying to make it all come together.

So for me, this is all a work in progress. I find a lot of mothers are in the
same boat. Women bear the burden of supporting activities at home, school,
work, community, church, and with family and friends. Without putting our
male counterparts down, many of them do not understand the depth of what
we do and go through to make the end results a reality. This is the work–life
balance.

Reverend Iyanla Vanzant was living in government housing projects
from 1970 to 1984 and got off public assistance when she attended law school.
But she was unpartnered, had kids, trying to make it all work. She says, "I
think work–life balance is a misnomer for an unpartnered mother raising
young children. That is a misnomer. What you have to do and how you have
to do it, all the emphasis is on making the money and providing for the kids.

If you can get a day or a couple of hours to yourself, that is about as balanced as you are going to get."

Marilyn Mosby, Baltimore City state's attorney, says that striking the right balance must also incorporate financial support of the family and the children. She offers this for today's mother, and future mothers, about success and providing for their families. Mosby says her mother once offered her this during a conversation: "Success is not measured by how much money you make, but by how you are passionate about what you are doing." That is something that stuck with me.

As a public servant, in her current position, Mosby acknowledges, "You don't make a lot of money. You do this because of your passion." But she believes ultimately the money will come. However, it is about her passion when she says she wants to "reform the system."

In the midst of it all, with her high-powered and demanding job, her Baltimore City Council husband, Nick Mosby, ran for mayor of the city; however, he dropped out of the race before the primaries. I can only imagine the intensity of that household, with two young children. But in her effort to balance the scales in her home, it is about giving her testimony of her struggles to her children. Mosby has also spoken of her mother's prior personal struggles with drugs. Mosby says, "As African American women, we don't share our testimonies enough. We don't share our experiences. We have become ashamed of our struggles that our children emulate and go through those same struggles. If we put our pride aside and really helped our children go through these issues, we would be better off. I experienced a lot of the struggles of life with my mother, and that helped me to make better decisions in life."

Since she has been in the position of Baltimore City state's attorney, her work-life balance has been "crazy." She continues to search for that balance. But she says what keeps her grounded is her faith. "At the end of the day this job is my passion. I love it. I am blessed every single day coming to work. But this is not hard. The hard job is the five- and seven-year-olds I go home to every day. That's the hard job and getting that right. Because at the end of the day I come home, from a very stressful day here, and I still have this little five-year-old stressing me, asking me, 'Where have you been?' It is story time. There is no sympathy for anything. She doesn't understand you have had a hard day. And doing that is the hard job."

Yet Mosby's example is shining through for her kids. Her daughter said to her one night when she had a lot of homework that when she grows up, "I want to be a mommy state's attorney." What touches Mosby's heart is the fact that she has put being a mother first before her official title. It's all about her motherhood.

Iyanla Vanzant says for working women and mothers, this concept of work-life balance is more for today than yesterday: "This is a very New-Age notion, work-life balance. My grandmother did not have no work-life balance! She scrubbed people's floors and cooked their food. And when her madam told her to come in at 5 o'clock in the morning, she got up and went and made that three dollars for the day! This work-life balance. Not saying that it is not important. But it goes back to culture."

She says there is time for balance: "You know where we get our balance is when three of us go shopping in the mall, even if we got the kids. We are dragging them kids along. That is when we get to talk and play and laugh and do what we do together as women. In this culture and society today, if I got two kids, and you got two kids, how am I going to help you? Unless we create it that way. And I think women are doing more of that. I hope they are doing more of that. 'Okay, this Saturday is yours, bring me all the kids.' 'Okay, you going to church. I'll be home this week. You do it next week.' We just have to learn how to cooperate with one another more and support one another. Again that goes back to culture. It goes back to culture. This is ancient, forgive me. When the men went out to hunt and they brought back the deer, the buffalo, the whatever, it was all those women came together around the fire or around wherever. They did the skinning and the cleaning and the sharing and the cutting up of the meat. That was community! Now we live in townhouses and condos, and we don't even speak to each other in the elevator."

It is about serving self, according to Vanzant: "It is about culture understanding. That we live in an 'I' dominated society. 'I. I. I. I am this!' 'I've got this degree.' 'I have got that.' But we are a 'we' people. We! And the way women, unpartnered women, mothers raising children alone or without a partner, the way that we are going to get back into balance is to begin to support one another in those ways."

Author Wes Moore reflects on his mother's efforts to gain support in one of the most trying times of her life. Moore says in amazement, "My mother is my angel." That angel, his mother, was "unprepared" as she instantly and "unexpectedly" became a widow, raising three kids on her own. Wes thinks about what it was like for his mom as she had to raise three children alone. Wes is now a parent like his mother and can only imagine her struggles as he raises his two children, a daughter and a son, with his wife. He is now living a parallel life as a parent, but not in her shoes, not walking in similar socioeconomic circumstances. He clearly remembers her struggle and keen understanding about support networks. When asked how it was to be a single mom, his mother would say, "In many ways, I wasn't." He recalls her saying, "Because I had no problem, I reached out to my parents. I reached out to my friends, I reached out to my minister. I reached out to whoever. If that meant something in some way to help my child, I was unabashed about it."

Moore remembers that the older his mother got, the more support she needed to seek out. The help she needed was very real. She moved to New York with her three children, two girls and Wes, who was the middle child and thirteen months older than his baby sister. Mrs. Moore moved in with her mother. She couldn't do it alone. She needed help, and she received it, but there were other concerns. At issue were the neighborhoods and the high murder rate in New York at the time. The only neighborhoods she could afford all had high crime and homicide rates. There were "certain distinct neighborhoods" like that. She had concerns about those areas and increasing fear and apprehension about other parts of society as her children were growing up quickly. Wes says, "My mother was always very clear she 'could not do this on her own.'"

First Lady Michelle Obama opened America's eyes to the realities of a working mother, a minority mother, stretched thin while giving the best to her job, which is to work on behalf of the citizens of this country, the world, and her husband and children. Mrs. Obama enlisted the help of her mother to "live above the store" for eight years and watch over Malia and Sasha. Iyanla Vanzant says the First Family's example is about "culture." The First Lady's natural instinct to have her mother, Mrs. Robinson, as her support is rooted in so many families across this country as a means to keep the values going and cut down on the expenses of childcare. But the way Vanzant views it, "The way things are in society today, the grandmothers are still working. You have thirty-five- and forty-year-old grandmothers, and they are still out working, and that creates a bit of a challenge. When I was growing up, my grandmother worked. She was the fallback guy. . . . I just appreciate what the First Lady did in saying, 'No nanny, no au pair, but my mother.'"

But now in 2016, Vanzant affirms, "It is more difficult for your average person because a grandmother could be thirty-five, and she is in the middle of her career, working out of the house the same as the mother is."

For me, Mrs. Obama was my mirror and made me smile when she came to the White House. I wanted my mother to care for my children, but she passed in May of 2007, never able to retire and do the things we had planned to do together. My hope was she would help watch my two daughters. That duty fell on my mother's sister, my Aunt Pearl, who for fourteen years has made it possible for me to work a dream, and an intensely stressful, job, packed with long hours. Yes, it is culture, but support too. That support was always compensated, but when you think of it, it would never match what my aunt, Mrs. Robinson, and other family members have given to our children. But that delicate balance could have created the most artful display or totally upset the apple cart of our lives.

Valerie Jarrett reiterates, it is all about that "network of support!" Reflecting on her personal story of divorce, "I was lucky because I felt both my parents were pulling for me." Even with the success and hard work her parents were having in their professional lives, they took time to make sure Valerie and her daughter were okay. They helped out. As Valerie was alone, her father had a daily ritual of transporting his granddaughter to school. Jarrett remembers, "Being a single mom, no matter how many resources you have and how much support you have, it's hard work. Being a mom is hard work. My parents lived a mile from me; my father came over every morning and took my daughter to school and picked her up from school, from the time she was in preschool to until she finished high school. So I had a huge support network from childhood to adulthood."

A lot of mothers have to do a self-examination of what is possible. Bishop Vashti McKenzie, the first female bishop of the AME Church, was named to that post in 2000. This was a significant moment in the church's two-hundred-year history. McKenzie found her reality on this subject, saying, "I think work-life balance was something that I thought was achievable and worked towards it for most of my career and my life until I realized there was no such thing as work-life balance. What it is, is priorities. And what is your priority? My kids, my husband. That's a priority. Other things can be delegated."

McKenzie was raised in a civic-minded and civil rights–focused family. Her grandmother was one of the founders of the African-American Greek sorority Delta Sigma Theta, and her family continues to champion the causes of the African American community, locally and nationally.

The realities of life many decades ago were simply a matter of survival for Blacks trying to sustain a family. But in those moments of survival, of feeding, clothing, and housing the family, many women forged a path we are all walking down now. California's 13th District Congresswoman Barbara Lee tearfully started our conversation for this book on the one-year anniversary of her mother's death, while she was driving to the cemetery to pay her respects. Lee said she and her mom, Mildred Parish Massey, went everywhere together. Her mother was blessed with longevity, suddenly dying at age ninety. Congresswoman Lee reflected on how she and her two sisters were raised to proudly understand they were Black and budding women and "just as equal as anyone else." Her mom was a feminist, a civil rights leader, and a trailblazer.

Mildred Massey was "the first for many." She was one of the first twelve students to integrate the University of Texas at El Paso. Mrs. Massey was the first African American woman civilian to work at Fort Bliss in Texas. She was also the first African American woman to work at the USO there. With love and admiration, Lee watched her mother push the boundaries in a racially charged Southern climate when it was not always accepted by the masses. Lee contends, "It was a fight and an uphill battle for her, but she never backed down." Massey broke "glass ceilings," as her daughter remembers from a very young age. "I grew up as a baby and then like two, three, and four years old, thinking that if she can do it, I can too. What is this, this thing about discrimination? Until I really realized when I started going to school and couldn't drink out of a water fountain."

The Black water fountains were designated with the sign "Colored" on them. Lee also remembers there were certain restaurants she could not patronize because of her skin color. Another painful fact for Lee, she remembers not being able to go to the movies with her Latino and White friends with whom she attended Catholic school because she was Black. She attended that school, understanding as early as age four that she was not attending public school because she was Black. There was a Black school available, yet her mother and grandfather decided against that experience, as they said they did not want to participate in any more segregation. She said, "All of that hit me." But her mom, and all she taught and lived, showed Lee, "I have got to figure out how to deal with this."

Taking a look back over her years, and her mother's influence, Lee said, "My whole life is about correcting injustices!" It's no surprise that years later, as an adult living in California, she worked as an activist. Lee was a "community worker" and got involved in the Black Panther Party in the late 1960s and early 1970s. What attracted her to it was its ten-point program of feeding kids, fighting for affordable housing, providing health care, and dealing with racism and discrimination. She corrects some and informs others about what the Panthers were. She says, "They weren't a nationalist party but a 'coalitions' party. Of people who were righteous and people who wanted justice, who wanted to change the system and not tinker around the edges."

She says, "The system has to be changed if you are going to deal with systemic racism. I was attracted to their [the Panthers'] method and their comprehensive approach to dealing with positive change in this country for poor people and for African Americans and for all people who were people of color who were low income and poor." She adds, "It was a natural progression."

Simultaneously she was the president of the Black Student Union at Mills College and was also the Northern California campaign coordinator for Shirley Chisholm in her campaign for president of the United States. Like their mother before them, Lee's sons watched her firsthand in her activism, particularly with the Black Panthers. She makes it known that in the 1970s, when she and her kids were there, her children "didn't see the guns" as they attended the political education classes taught by Bobby Seale. Lee wanted her sons to learn about what a movement was, "so they would grow up to have a social consciousness and what justice was all about." Her children traveled with her everywhere. She was on public assistance and in school. She could not afford to hire a babysitter. So her children learned with her about how to effect change and about advocacy for the people. Her kids learned volunteerism at the ages of four and five as they attended survival rallies and had the job of bagging groceries for the underserved. They also sold the Black Panther newspaper.

A mother's influence is strong. Her words and deeds are profound. Actress and businesswoman Victoria Rowell descends from the *Mayflower*, as her mother, Dorothy Rowell, is of English origin. Rowell is still looking for her birth father who she believes is a Jamaican Black man. But she reflects on her foster parents, including the foster mother who instilled in her a work and business ethic. Robert and Agatha Armstead, a Black couple, were Rowell's primary foster family, after a temporary placement with a White family ended when Victoria was two-and-a-half years old. Rowell was born from a mixed-race coupling. The highly acclaimed actress, while researching her life story, learned it was illegal in sixteen states for White families to take a Black child at that time. The Taylor family, a White progressive family, wanted Victoria and kept her until a Black foster family was found.

Agatha Armstead was well educated and supported the arts. She was one of four sisters who mirrored one another in their upwardly mobile social, business, and economic ways of thinking. They also understood "the anchoring effects of the arts." Agatha, Rowell's foster mother, was born in 1903, and Rowell said she was like a "grandmother-mother to me!" The Armsteads were foster parents to ten other children before she came to live with them. The family owned a farmhouse in Maine and homes in Massachusetts. Mrs. Armstead saved her money for their sixty-acre Maine retirement home through what Rowell calls her "Rosie the Riveter savings" from the 1940s. Mrs. Armstead's influence and work ethic are evident in Rowell, who acknowledges, "There was an importance of owning property. It was a primary focus of mine in Hollywood."

Rowell is a multiple-property owner who contends that not many Blacks to this day own a home in the Hollywood Hills, but she does. She proudly boasts ownership of her 1923 Mediterranean home. Victoria Rowell celebrates her foster mother's successes and what she taught her, especially as she was three generations from slavery and left a plantation in North Carolina to climb the economic and social ladders of success. Mrs. Armstead's determination in the midst of it all is inspiring. Early on with her life with Rowell, Mrs. Armstead had a body-deforming mastectomy and was told she could not lift the baby. Defying the doctors, Mrs. Armstead did.

And the rest is history.

· 10 ·

Educating the Future

"*Value!*"

After all that has been said in these chapters, I am left with the word *value*. It struck me after Bishop Vashti McKenzie addressed it, and then my thoughts were reaffirmed with President Barack Obama's words. He eloquently spoke of it from his unique perch, the highest office in the land, sitting as the forty-fourth president of the United States of America.

As adults we crave and pursue being valued and continue on endless and countless journeys to find the meaning in our lives. It once again comes back to value. If we as adults are going through this exercise on value, imagine how children are affected. Children look to us for so many reasons that include feeling reassured and valued. We are the first teacher of that feeling and concept that must eventually exude from their being.

Motherhood is a spiritual awakening and a manifestation of a better self for the care and upbringing of the next generations, who have the benefit of our wisdom and experience to navigate the waters successfully. But when motherhood is absent, it is obvious and painful. Reverend Iyanla Vanzant says, "When you meet someone who has not had the magic, if you will, the beauty, the glory of a mother's love, there is a piece of them that is just missing."

Mothers are crucial, but there is more to the equation in raising a child. As the African proverb states, it takes a village. Joshua DuBois, a new father and President Barack Obama's spiritual advisor and former head of the Faith Based and Neighborhood Partnerships office, supports President Obama's prescription for raising kids. He offers his personal prescription on what should happen. "I would actually speak to those surrounding mothers and say that we need to step up as men and fathers and do more to make sure our women do not have to carry these emotional burdens on their own."

While there is a call for men to step up, many households are headed by a single parent, mostly women with children. So when it comes to the emotional responsibilities of mothers, Judge Mablean Ephriam of the TV show *Justice with Judge Mablean* feels it is a mother's "responsibility to teach children the ways of the world and the ways of the Lord. . . . They set the tone."

Ephriam said, "It sounds cliché, but we have to get back to the community raising the children, the village. We have got to get back to having a neighborhood . . . a real community. In these mixed neighborhoods we have to become neighbors to each other. It can't be 'I live over here but I don't have anything to do with you and you don't have anything to do with me.'" She finds the innocence of children could be the answer. "Fortunately, if you leave children alone and you put them outside, they are going to play together and they are going to be able to play with each other. But when the parents get in the mix and say, 'I don't want you playing with. . . .' Until the adults in the neighborhood and the parents in the neighborhood say that 'we are going to be parents and this is going to be a neighborhood where we are going to be concerned about each other and we are going to teach our children how they should love and treat each other,' not only are we going to teach them, we are going to show them because we are going to be the first example."

She also encourages people to become consciously aware of these "attitudes about race," going as far as to say the "prevailing attitudes" permeate everywhere, from the schoolhouse to the public square. But to look hard, she says we have to be honest with ourselves about our own thoughts about different groups.

The evolution on matters of race and mothers involves more than just private citizens. Valerie Jarrett says, "Post-Obama who will Black America be? We are just going to have to continue plugging away, working hard, doing right by our families. . . . We are strong, and we are determined, and we have a lot of heart, and that is to our advantage. And I think that we will continue to do right by our children to give them every possible opportunity. I think the fact that the President and First Lady have been beacons of hope, not just because they are African American, so many young people can relate to their story and see themselves through their eyes in a sense. . . . So when the First Lady sits down with some high school girls and talks about what it was like to go to public high school in Chicago and have never heard of Princeton and the only reason she heard of it is because her brother Craig played basketball there, and have a college counselor tell her 'You can't possibly get in a good school,' but yet apply, succeed, and do well and go on to Harvard. That is such a positive role model for these young people."

A piece of the puzzle that needs to be in the overall equation is that history is embraced along with the understanding that the rights struggle is not over. The further away we get from the Civil Rights Movement of the 1950s and 1960s, there is more of a sense of accomplishment that sometimes negates a struggle. That false sense of victory prevents us from thinking about the work that is left, the racial gaps that remain to be closed.

Congresswoman Barbara Lee wants us not to forget who we are realistically, urging us, "Don't forget your history and don't forget your past. Understand that African American women still, when you look at income inequality, I think we are still at the bottom of the barrel. When you look at unemployment rates, when you look at caregivers, we don't get a tax credit for being a caregiver. We are the majority of caregivers. When you look at the economic status of African American women and when you look at the political clout we have and power, I think we are the most loyal Democrats in the country. We have to be proud, first of all, of our history and know our history. But also, women moving forward have to understand that there are some real systemic issues that affect African American women."

Lee is convinced that "We are the soul of this country!" She says it is about that Ghanaian idea of the Sankofa Experience. "In order to move forward you have to look back. You have to know your history, you have to understand the mistakes that were made, and you are able to move forward and solve problems and see the future as it should be." Lee believes Black women embody the Sankofa Experience. "With all the challenges we have we are still at it. Young Black women have got to keep it going. That is the only way this country is gonna change." She goes on to say, "Black women like Harriet Tubman, Sojourner Truth, Ida B. Wells, Shirley Chisholm, and Fannie Lou Hamer, they are the ones who led this country in a chorus that required liberty and justice for all, and we still haven't gotten there yet."

With the inequities of the future that still face the Black community and with Black women owning such political clout, there should be a demand to be at the table to craft policies to better the condition of this community. The absence of our voice at the table has resulted in generations of a downward spiral that continues to keep us out of the solution process, without a seat at the table. Shirley Chisholm said if they don't have a seat at the table for you, bring the folding chair when you get to the table. We have power as Black women and Black mothers. Our power is distinct and should be courted. In 2013 the Republican Party created the *Growth and Opportunity Report* after the Republican Party lost the Black vote in the 2012 presidential election. The GOP lost Black women by 97 percent to 3 percent and Hispanic women by 81 percent to 19 percent. They need the minority vote. So why haven't we understood that we have leveraging power? We have power, but it all goes back to understanding our value.

Chairman of the Republican National Committee Reince Priebus has a bit more understanding on the diversity issue than one might assume. He once worked at the NAACP Legal Defense Fund in Los Angeles, California, and learned about racial acceptance from his mother who grew up in Khartoum, Sudan. Priebus offered some frank revelations on the statistics of Black women. He said, "W have to understand in our party [that] women of color are the fastest growing voting bloc in America. Understanding that means that we need to speak to women of color, Black women, on a regular basis."

The hope of better days and a plan to reverse this downward spiral may be here. As we look at fixing the existing problems, there is hope for a much brighter day. Iconic activist Harry Belafonte says, "I am awakened at eighty-nine to these young people." In his evening years, he is seeing that the fight for equality is not over, understanding that "our classic institutions are not able to rally the citizens around protests and mobilization so that will change the course of social behavior. Our institutions have failed us. I am absolutely delighted some of these young people are taking these matters into their own hands."

With each child that is born there is the wonder of life and then the hope this new life will be the one to make a transition into White society. But again, that effort stems from the supportive role, words, and actions of a mother. Reverend Iyanla Vanzant steps up, saying we are the first teacher, and "the job is to nourish, nurture, and educate." But Iyanla falls back on culture and community, saying we all have a responsibility in raising children.

Coincidently, the name Iyanla means "great mother." With that name and its meaning comes great responsibility as she feels the calling to "mother" not just for her own children, but those with whom she comes in contact. But in our effort to be mothers to our children and reverse the downward cycles for kids, Vanzant's philosophy has a broad reach beyond the focus on just our own. She says, "It is about mothering people," and she also says she does not have to know you. "You are my child whether you are fourteen or forty or fifty because I understand what it means to be a mother." Overall, on the topic of a prescription for mothers and the community as a whole, the prescription for dealing with matters of race, Vanzant says, "We need to call it out and we need to deal with it and we don't need people to agree with us that it exists. I think that is a mother's job. Not to get mad about it and fuss about it and talk about it, but to say to people, 'Are you aware the way you are speaking to me right now is considered racist?'"

Value and respect are components to our interactions in teaching others how we must be treated. The example comes from Maryland Congressman Elijah Cummings and his mother. He remembers what she taught him when he was a child. That memory came back during a highly publicized time in his life when the head of the Oversight and Government Reform Committee, Darrell Issa, turned Cummings's microphone off, preventing his voice from being heard during a May 2014 televised Capitol Hill hearing on the IRS scandal. Issa rudely cut off Cummings's microphone because he wanted to close the session and not allow Cummings to follow up and question those testifying at the hearing. When the incident happened, Cummings thought of his mother's words, "You have to teach them how to treat you!" For Cummings, that childhood lesson "that was taught to me over sixty years ago" is very relevant today. Issa eventually apologized for his actions after the groundswell of concern and outrage that became a huge news story broadcast around the world. Cummings says of his mother, her wisdom on matters to include race surpassed her fifth-grade education. He considers his mom a "brilliant" human being.

But ultimately, a child needs to unquestionably know and feel love to feel his or her own value and self-worth.

Gwen Carr, the mother of Eric Garner, the man who died in police custody in New York City on July 17, 2015, had a heart for children, as she raised her three and her late brother's children in an effort not to separate his trio. At one point she had six kids in the house. She was a widowed mother of three herself after her husband died at the age of thirty-three of high blood pressure–related issues. Carr was in her late twenties and left to raise a five-year-old, a four-year-old, and a four-month-old at the time of his death. Then a few years later her sister-in-law and then her brother died in the 1980s. Her family ultimately did not want to break up her brother's kids, so she took them in. She was a single parent who received some financial and disciplinary help from her parents. But with the packed household and the demands of daily life, she proudly acknowledged she had one job and "never put them on welfare." She was a train operator with the New York City Transit Authority and before that she was a postal worker, but by trade she is trained as an accountant. She credits "the grace of God" for helping her raise the children. Ultimately she remarried and helped raise stepchildren and even took in a girl from the community. But despite all of her success in raising so many children, she ultimately lost two of her own in violent ways.

Actress Victoria Rowell does not negate the power of love, saying it is "in huge deficit." Rowell, a mother herself and once a foster child heavily influenced by her foster mother and her foster family, says *love* is an action word. "We can teach love, we can show love, love is something that is taught by example." Our love example is exhibited in our strength, as she says we are strong and not fragile. "We are not furniture, and we don't fall apart." Rowell says our roles are varied. "A mother is a big sister, a mother is an auntie, a mother is a grandmother, a mother is all of what women are. A mother is a teacher, a mentor."

We wear so many hats and shoulder the responsibility of shaping lives. Looking at the statistics, Black women are valuable because we bear the brunt of the majority of negatives in this country. Yet to our credit, once we walk in our truth and fully embrace our value, we can and will birth the generations and shape thoughts that can help our community finally evolve in racial parity. Rowell affirms, "Without us there will be no procreation, and the weight is on us how children's lives are affected." I can't help but think of President Obama's Howard University commencement speech in May 2016, when he referenced some of the most prolific writers of our time, in relation to Rowell's comments. If you really think about it, mothers shape the generations to build and fulfill what Lorraine Hansberry wrote about being in the book *To Be Young, Gifted and Black*. Once we walk in our truth, we can chart our destiny as depicted in the 1937 novel by Zora Neale Hurston, *Their Eyes Were Watching God*.

But as we hope for a glass half full on matters of racial equality and first-class citizenship, we must see reality, the reality of what Langston Hughes wrote during the Harlem Renaissance, "Life ain't no crystal stair," in his poem "Mother to Son." Broderick Johnson, the Baltimore native who was chosen to head President Obama's My Brother's Keeper initiative, says, "Race still matters greatly in this country. And it is important to help our children understand it does still matter a great deal. You can't wish it away. But we have to, as my parents did, prepare ourselves for achieving in the face of it. And that to me means taking advantage of opportunities that you can give your children and make sure they know they have to take those opportunities and work hard at whatever it is before them. And let them not forget where they came from."

A Prayer for Harmony

ife is pregnant with possibilities. One of those possibilities is a day when inequality is a thing of the past and we can truly say we are a postracial society, one that is minus overt and subtle racism. We are forward-looking and forward-moving people who are hopeful about budding promises and potentials life has to offer. I equate this to a view of hope to the creation of life. If you have ever talked to expecting parents, you understand. For the most part, expectant and new mothers are anxious but have such hopes for their unborn, and then continue to want the best for them, no matter the reality and condition of their lives. That baby that is growing in the womb of that mother is thought of as the hope of tomorrow.

But as we see the good in that scenario, there is a flip side that is ugly. Iyanla Vanzant said "when you meet someone who has not had the magic, if you will, the beauty, the glory of a mother's love, there is a piece of them that is just missing." The bonding of mother and child begins when the fetus is in the womb. The first thing you heard was your mother's heartbeat. That was your connection to life. And the next thing you heard was her voice. As mothers, that physical metamorphosis creates a spiritual link, a bonding that makes women want the best for their children, even before they meet them on delivery day.

The hope materializes through words. In many cases those words are sent to the ears of a higher power to open hearts and change conditions. Prayer is nothing more than talking to God of hopes and expectations, giving thanks, and even questioning why. The prayers have resounded in the Black church for decades. In today's Black churches, the message is the meeting of the social issues of the day and the word of God. In other houses of worship the same holds true, making the message relevant to the masses.

When Harry Belafonte was a little boy, his mother found ample need for prayer. He remembers "constantly on my mother's lips were utterances that suggest that we should bring an end to injustice, to poverty, to unemployment, to racial issues. That was a constant on her lips . . . I think that had it not been for her commitment and her insightfulness on how to manage these challenges that came her way, I would have never been able to find my way into this space doing the things that I do, in this space in which I do it. I hold her wonderfully responsible for the better part of who I am."

But there are others who find the answers in other forms. Should there be a prayer for harmony in this country? Reverend Iyanla Vanzant says, "I don't believe we need prayer."

Erika Alexander is young in years but wise in her ways of creating bonds of sister- and auntie-hood for many women. By e-mail she said of the prayer for racial harmony, "I am spiritual, but I do not pray for racial harmony. How does that prayer start off anyway? 'Please God stop White people from hating us poor Black folks?' LOL. I do not pray like that, but I, like most, am exhausted and over-grieved with the monotony of racial disharmony. So to offset the frustration that I feel, I work. I also work very hard to be excellent, hoping my work and results can make the difference. So yes, prayer may work for some, but I'd rather wage a campaign of enlightenment by provoking or writing a project that changes the hearts and minds of racists in the slyest way, by harnessing the human need to feel good. To be in harmony."

African Americans are an accepting people who were made so because it was in part a means of survival. Another part of that equation was faith and prayers. But I am hearing more and more that it is not about prayer. It is about the work.

Actress Rae Dawn Chong contends, "Faith and prayer are useless; otherwise we would have no hardship. Sorry, but petitioning has never brought results. Results come when we raise our inner vibration and include all. So as a species we are fear-driven and faithless, so that is why we have a culture that worships money above all else and will probably be the end of our era and civilization. Tragically the greed that pervades society is the force that prevents harmony and community. This is a country of proud ignoramuses. We are considering Trump as a potential president, and this alone reflects the blind ignorance and greed and xenophobia that pervades Middle America. I think it is called 'wetiko,' a soul sickness of greed, an actual mental soul spiritual sickness. I laugh because the architects of this valueless way of life are billionaires, but if there isn't a planet and a healthy populace, who cares if you have a lot of money? You will have nothing to do or people to see. We are simple, we need love. That is it. We need community, and being racially divided does not provide security or peace. Trump and his followers know better, and yet do they? Dumb America is scary. Racist America is fear based, and we somehow must go back to our essence as kindhearted, loving, inclusive beings. Racial harmony is harmony, nothing on the planet of guns and fear is harmonious. All war is for money, money is for safety. I say be loving and safe and end all war."

The evolution of racial issues in this country and racism are evident, from slavery to Jim Crow laws to the civil rights movement to 1992, when we saw the first racial riots in decades happen after the Rodney King verdict. From the time enslaved Africans were brought to this country, there has been some form of discriminatory behavior and/or actions against the Black community. One of the main problems this country now witnesses is that the Black community, once the majority-minority group in this country, has been placed on the back burner when it comes to racial groups in this nation. The ranking and status for change diminished as Hispanics took the number-one spot as the majority-minority group in this country.

Also, a huge problem, in my humble opinion, is we have dropped the blueprint that our "talented tenth" as popularized in the essay by W.E.B. DuBois. That blueprint is the civil rights movement. Every group from the LGBT community to the women's rights community to the Hispanic community has picked up that blueprint. We have forgotten it, and now we are suffering the consequences of not taking action against issues that negatively impact us. But people looked to "hope" and "change" as if the Savior were coming back. Valerie Jarrett is reminded of a saying from Dr. King: "I think the arc of the moral universe is long but it does bend toward justice." She also has the conviction, over the past couple of years in particular, that there has now been a spotlight on the fact that we still have extraordinary inequity in this country. And we still have discrimination and racism. That shouldn't come as any surprise! None of us should be under any illusion that just by electing an African American U.S. president, generations of the legacy of racism were going to evaporate overnight.

We all can take responsibility. That includes the average American to the highest elected officials of this land for change or the lack of change on the racial front in 2017 and beyond in this, the greatest country in the world. We don't march as much anymore. I find as a journalist, the squeaky wheel gets the oil. A consistent, persistent galvanized movement that marches and brings attention can cause the wheels of change to start its slow move, but movement nonetheless. We don't do that anymore. Why? Who knows?

It could be a lot of reasons—fear of change, fear of losing what you have worked for, or simple complacency. With all of these ideas, what can move the mountain? A miracle! What is the prayer for harmony, if there is one?

Faith without work is dead! But to pray is faith that closed hearts and minds would be open to that which you request of a higher power. Matters of race deal with the heart, and as the Bible says, "As a man thinketh so is he." It is the moral issue of our time yet again. Well, let me correct that statement; it never stopped being a moral imperative. The landscape of race just changes every few years. But if we pray to or make a request of a higher power, what would we ask or should we even ask?

Everyone has a different approach to fighting the good, hard battle of the hundreds-year-old problem of the racial divide in this country. When we think of race, we are hypersensitive about the matter. Why? The answer to that 1,000-pound question can only be answered on an individual basis. For Whites as well as Blacks and other races of people, we must search our minds and hearts for the answer to that question and then we can begin to tackle, in a systemic way, the subtle and overt racism that haunts this country. Prayers are words or a word spoken to a higher power to open the heart and possibly change the soul. I do pray for racial harmony, but I also practice what I want. The higher power we call on for moral direction offers love. *Love* is the action word that can turn it all around. In the 1950s and 1960s Black churches were the backdrop of that effort to change hearts during the speeches and rallies against injustice. In Charleston, South Carolina, love was ever-present when that White gunman opened fire on the nine people in Mother Emanuel Church.

What we love about ourselves as a country is what we now hate and fear. We welcome diversity and then push it away. Lady Liberty stood offering a beacon of hope to so many from other countries. But for people of my ancestry, they only saw the belly of a ship if they survived the journey from the motherland. Yes, I pray so my heart is not hardened when I think about the treatment of my ancestors in this country. I pray that God offers me the right words to say when people tell me I am a "race baiter" or when facts and statistics are our proof that we have not yet received equality or first-class citizenship.

Anytime you have to enact a law on matters of race to correct wrongs, you know there are still problems. After I pray, what I am left with is a simple question for my fellow Americans of other communities who dare me on matters of race. My question to you, with the reporting at the White House out of the equation and all the things that go along with that, is would you like to trade places with me and live my Black existence?

And the answer is . . . ?

Acknowledgments

$\mathscr{I}$ want to acknowledge my two daughters, Ryan and Grace, who have been my inspiration since their birth. Thank you to my late mother for being an exceptional example of motherhood, perseverance, grace, and elegance.

I want to thank my Aunt Pearl, who has helped raise my girls for almost fifteen years. Your invaluable help has allowed me to do what I do every day. Thank you to my family members who have gone to heaven since the last book. Your belief in me is the wind beneath my wings. We miss you! Thank you to my family for the love and support. To my friends who support me and pretend to understand when I can't go out because I am home with the kids or writing a book!

Thank you to all the women who have mothered and poured into me. Your spirit is in these pages. Thank you!

To my team, thank you again on a job well done. Diane Nine, my agent, and Dave Smitherman, my editor, and Ted Randler for the painting of my girls.

To Audra and David, thank you both.

To Rowman & Littlefield, thanks for believing in me again for book number two.

To all those who participated in this book project, thank you for offering your heart. I am floored by the honest conversations you allowed me to share in this book.

President Obama, thank you for participating a second time in my book project. You don't know what it means! I will relish your words and contributions in this book and in my first book, *The Presidency in Black and White*, forever.

President Carter, thank you for honoring me with your memories of your mother. I am more than humbled.

Thank you, God, to whom all things are possible. Habakkuk 2:2: "Write the vision, and make it plain upon tablets, that he may run that readeth it."

Index

Photos are indicated by *p1*, *p2*, etc.

African American Women, town hall of, 39. *See also* Black women
Afro, cultural assimilation and, 102–3
Air Force One, 14–16
Alexander, Erika, 55, 99, 105–6, 124
AME Church, 114
American Urban Radio Network, 79
Angelou, Maya, 62
Anne of Green Gables, 77
assimilation, 99–107; Belafonte on, 103–4; conformity and, 99; cultural, 102–3; diversity concerns, 103–4; doll test and, 99–101; race-based, 105; Vanzant's white attire and, 104–5
aunt and uncle, shooting incident involving, 94–98

Baker, Ella, 27–28
Baltimore, 87–98; areas of, 87, 88–89; as city of survival, 94; dual world syndrome, 95; Moore on, 91–93; Pennsylvania Avenue, 88–89; Walbrook Junction shooting, 94–98
Baltimore riots, 2; locale and surrounding neighborhoods, 87, 88–89; personal experience of, 35–36; "the talk" and, 10, 11, 12; truck driver with Confederate flag, 11–12, 36; viral video of Graham and son, 38
beauty shop politics, 82
Behar, Joy, 51
Belafonte, Harry, 58, 70, 103–4, 124; on future and fight for equality, 120; mother of, 71–72
Belcher, Cornell, 18
Bellafanti, Melvine, 71
Bethlehem Steel, 87–88
Bible, 65, 75, 76, 80, 126. *See also specific scriptures*
bitch, 60
Black America, post-Obama, 118
Black children, 65–66; doll test on self-esteem of, 99–101; expulsion rates for minority preschoolers, 43; perceived threat of teenage girls, 42
Black churches, 114, 126; prayer in, 123; in support of King, M. L. Jr., 69
Black community: civil rights focus in, 114; n-word and, 56–57; self-esteem issues in, 100–101; "the talk" and, 5–9; work-life support in, 112–13
Blacklash, 18
Black men, missing, 24–25

Black Panther Party, 115–16
Blackting (acting), 106
Black women, 39; as change agents, 82; in Congress, 17; earning statistics, 22–23; invisibility issue for, 19–21; marriage and divorce statistics on, 28; missing, 24–25; objectification of, 42; omissions in history, 26–27; percentage of US population, 24–25
Bloody Sunday, 48, 51
Bolton Hill, 87
Booker, Caroline Jordan, 25–26
Booker, Cory, 24, 25–26, 27, 43, 58–59
book tour, 9–10, 32–33; restaurant incident during, 13–14
Boston Review, 24
Bowman, James E., 30
BridgeEdU, 91
Brooks, Cornell, 51
Brown, Michael, 6, 39
Brown vs. Board of Education, 8, 99–100, 101
Bundles, A'Lelia, 82–83
Bush, George W., 29, 82

Canada, 106
Capehart, Jonathan, 50
Carr, Gwen, 37–38, 121
Carson, Ben, 50
Carter, Jimmy, 84–85
Carter, Lillian (mother of Carter, J.), 84–85
cell phone cameras, 40
Center for Global Policy Solutions, 23
Chicago Housing Authority, 30
Chicago police force, 73
children: mothers impact on, 65–66; Obama, 55, 113; percentage of minority, 66. *See also* Black children
Chisholm, Shirley, 17–18, 115
Chong, Rae Dawn, 55–56, 72–73, 106; on greed, and prayer, 124–25
Circle of Mothers, 72
Civil Rights Act, 9, 57, 93

civil rights activism, work-life balance and, 114
Civil Rights Movement, 118–19; Black Panther Party, 115–16; faith and, 68, 70, 75–77; mothers of, 43–44, 68, 70
Clinton, Hillary Rodham, 73–75
Clinton, William Jefferson (Bill), 67, 103, *p8*
Clyburn, James, 81
Colbert, Stephen, 54
Cole, Michael, 77–78
community, work-life balance and, 112–13. *See also* Black community
Condon, George, 52
Confederate flag, 10, 11–12, 36, 49
Congress, first Black woman in, 17
Congressional Black Caucus Legislative Week, 2015, 74
The Cosby Show, 99
criminal justice reform, 40–41
culture: cultural assimilation, 102–3; work-life balance and, 112
Cummings, Elijah, 75–76, 100–101; on assimilation and integration, 107; on Baltimore, 88; microphone incident with Issa, 120–21

Daily News, 51–52
Darden, Christopher, 21–22, 60–61
Darden, Marvie (mother of Darden, C.), 22, 60–62
daughters: Obama, 55, 113. *See also* Grace; Ryan
Demo Day, 7
discrimination, housing, 26
diversity, assimilation and, 103–4
divorce, 28, 30–31
Dodson, Milo, 47–48
dolls: childhood, 101, 102; doll test, 99–101
dreadlocks, 105
Drew, Charles, 2
Driving While Black (DWB), 5
dual world syndrome, 95

DuBois, Joshua, 69, 117
DuBois, W. E. B., 83, 125
Dunham, Stanley Ann (mother of Obama, B.,), 85–86
DWB. *See* Driving While Black

Earnest, Josh, 52–55, 94
Ellington, Duke, 52
Ellison, Ralph Waldo, 19
Ephriam, Mablean, 37, 56, 100, 107, 118
equality, 81; hope and reality of, 122; youth fight for, 120
executive orders, 82
expulsion rates, for minority preschoolers, 43

faith: civil rights movement and, 68, 70, 75–77; connection between race and mothers', 65–80; Ryan, A., mother's death and, 79–80
Faith-Based Initiative, 69
family leave, 24
fathers, "the talk" given by, 5–9
foster parents, 116, 121
Freedom Riders, 44
FUBU, 7
Fulton, Jahvaris, 72
Fulton, Sybrina, 8, 36, 44, 72
future, 117–22

Garner, Eric, 6, 37–38, 121
gestation, mother's impact on child during, 65–66
Gilliard, Martha (aunt of Ryan, A.), 94–98
Goldberg, Whoopi, 51
Gowans Ryan, Mary Vivian (mother of Ryan, A.), 28, 78–80, *p1–p4*, *p8*; work and life of, 109–10
Grace (younger daughter of Ryan, A.), 10, 11, 32–33, *p7*, *p8*; Baltimore riots and, 35–36; birth of, 79; with Clinton, B., *p6*; doll chosen by, 102; with Obamas, *p5*

Gray, Freddie, 6, 10–11, 14; funeral of, 90; mother's love and, 39
"great mother," 120
greed, 124–25
Growth and Opportunity Report, 119

Hamer, Fannie Lou, 27, 119
harmony, prayer and, 123–26
Hispanic women, earning statistics for, 23
history, women in, 17; Black mothers' path in, 42; Black women omission in, 26–27
Hollywood Hills, 116
Homeland Security, 6
housing, 30; discrimination, 26; projects, in civil rights-era Selma, 44
Hughes, Langston, 44–45, 122
human genome, 103

identity, mother's reinforcement of, 102
incarceration, mass, 41
integration, 114–15; Cummings on assimilation and, 107; Ephriam on negative impact of, 107; in schools, 98
Internet, police shootings and, 6
interviews: with Earnest, 53–55; with Graham, 39; with Obama, B., 14–16, 41
invisibility issue: for Back women, 19–21; missing Black men and women, 24–25
Issa, Darrell, 77, 120–21

Jackson, Andrew, 50
James, book of, 75
Japanese Americans, during World War II, 74
Jarrett, Valerie, 15–16, 29, 60, 113–14; on invisibility issue, 20–21; on n-word, 49; on police encounter, 93–94; on post-Obama Black America, 118; on racism, 125; on

statistics, 30–31; on viral video of, 38; on walks with Obama, M., 20
jigaboo, 51
John, Daymond, 7
Johnson, Broderick, 89–91, 122
Johnson, Hannah, 82
Johnson, Jeh, 6
Johnson, Lyndon B., 84

King, Don, 62–63
King, Martin Luther, Jr., 9, 68, 71, 103–4; Clinton, H., and, 74–75; president legislating holiday in honor of, 83; support from Black churches, 69
King, Rodney, 125
Ku Klux Klan (KKK), 83

language: Dodson on n-word and, 47–48; linguistic ideologies, 48
LA Unified School District, 77
Lee, Barbara, 114–15, 119
Legal Defense Fund, NAACP, 120
Leonhardt, David, 7, 24
leukemia, 3
Lewis, John Robert, 8–9, 43–44; parents of, 67–71
Lewis, Willa Mae, 8, 67–69, 70
Lilly Ledbetter Fair Pay Act, 40
Limbaugh, Rush, 51
Lincoln, Abraham, 82
London, 9–10, 32–33
London Eye, *p7*
love, as action word, 126
Love, Loni, 58, 102–3
love, mother's, 35–45; faith, religion and, 65; Graham's actions and, 36–39; healing power of, 40; Hughes' poem on, 44–45; Vanzant on, 36
lynching, 83

majority-minority status, 66–67
Mandela, Nelson, 103–4
"Marriage and Divorce Patterns by Gender, Race and Educational Attainment," 28

Martin, Trayvon, 6, 7–8, 36, 44, 72
Maryland State Police, 11
Massey, Mildred, 114–15
mass incarceration, 41
Matthew, book of, 77
McAuliffe, Terry, 94
McGill, Hogan (uncle of Ryan, A.), 94–98
McKenzie, Vashti, 41–43, 65, 80, 114, 117; on Penn Central, 88–89
McLeod Bethune, Mary, 27
media, 6, 39, 40
mentorship, 43
microphone incident, Cummings and Issa, 120–21
minorities: expulsion rates among preschoolers, 43; majority-minority statistics, 66; majority-minority status, 66–67
MIT, 29
The Mod Squad, 62, 77–78
Moore, Wes, 38–39, 59–60, 91–93; on mother's work and life, 112–13
Moreno, Carolina, 66–67
Morgan, Garrett, 2
Mosby, Marilyn, 98, 99, 111
Mosby, Nick, 111
Moses, 42
Mother Emanuel Church, 126
mothers: of civil rights movement, 43–44, 68, 70; of Clinton, H., 73–75; conspiring by, 43; expectant and new, 123; future hope and challenges, 117–22; identity reinforcement by, 102; impact on children, 65–66; instincts of, 3–4; job of, 1, 11; loss of own, 3–4, 28; of Martin, 7–8, 44, 72; of Obama, B., 85–86; path in history of Black, 42; presidents, race and, 81–86; as primary earners, 7, 110; protective instinct of, 39; race, faith and, 65–80; race discussion with, 1–2; roles of, 121–22; single, 7, 23, 31, 110, 118; spiritual experience of motherhood,

73; statistics on single, 23; support needed by, 112–13; unpartnered, 110–11, 112; work-life balance for, 109–16. *See also* love, mother's; "the talk"; *specific women*
My Brother's Keeper, 86, 89, 122

NAACP, 50, 51, 120, *p1*
Nash, Diane, 28
Neale Hurston, Zora, 122
New York Times, 6, 7, 24
"990 People Shot Dead by Police in 2015," 42
n-word (*nigger/nigga*), 47–63; Black community and, 56–57; Blacks' use of, 57; Booker, Cory on, 58–59; Carter's mother opposing, 85; dictionary origins of, 60–61; Dodson on language and, 47–48; doll test and, 100; Jarrett on, 49; Obama, Malia and, 55; Reshaping ideology and, 48; response to Wilmore's use of, 50–51; Wilmore's use of, 49–55

Obama, Barack, 6, 18, 19, 29, 32, 117, *p5*, *p6*; achievements during administration of, 40; Black America after, 118; commencement speech in 2016, 122; daughters of, 113; Demo Day, 7; Faith-Based Initiative, 69; interview aboard *Air Force One*, 14–16; interview on criminal justice reform, 41; Jarrett and, 31; mother of, 85–86; response to Wilmore use of n-word, 53–55; on soul and truth, 66; use of n-word by, 48–49
Obama, Barack, Sr., 85
Obama, Malia (daughter of Obamas), 55, 113
Obama, Michelle, 32, 113, 118, *p5*; invisibility issue and, 19–20; walks taken by, 19–20
Obama, Sasha (daughter of Obamas), 113

objectification, 42
O'Malley, Martin, 87
"1.5 Million Missing Black Men," 7, 24
Oversight and Government Reform Committee, 120–21

parenthood, as sacred, 4
Parks, Rosa, 56
passion, success as, 111
Pennsylvania Avenue, 88–89
Pinckney, Clementa, 10
Planas, Roque, 66–67
Plante, Bill, 51
police, 11; Jarrett's encounter with, 93–94; videotaping, of confrontations with, 40
police force, Chicago, 73
police shootings, 5; accountability and, 40; Fulton, J., 72; Garner, 6, 37–38, 121; Gray, 6, 10–11, 14, 39, 90; Internet and, 6; London awareness of, 9–10; in media, 6, 39; "990 People Shot Dead by Police in 2015," 42. *See also* Baltimore riots
politics, beauty shop, 82
Poor People's Campaign, 88
population, US, 21, 24–25
post-Obama, Black America, 118
poverty, 23
prayer, harmony and, 123–26
pregnancies, 36
preschoolers, expulsion rates among minority, 43
The Presidency in Black and White (Ryan, A.), 5, 9–10
presidents, mothers, race and, 81–86. *See also specific presidents*
President's Committee on Equality of Treatment and Opportunity, 81
President's Initiative on Race, 67
Priebus, Reince, 10, 19, 119–20
primary earners, 7, 110
princess incident, 32–33
Pryor, Richard, 57–58

Quealy, Kevin, 7, 24

race and racism: in Canada, 106; current spotlight on, 125; discussions with mother on, 1–2; as heart issue, 2; as moral issue, 76–77; mothers, faith and, 65–80; mothers, presidents and, 81–86; President's Initiative on Race, 67; race-based assimilation, 105; restaurant incident, 13
racial harmony, 125
racial profiling, 5
Reagan, Jack (father of Reagan, R.), 84
Reagan, Ronald, 83
The Real, 58
religion: mothers' love, race and, 65–80; Yoruba, 104
Republican National Committee (RNC), 10
Reshaping ideology, 48
restaurant incident, during book tour, 13–14
revolution, women's, 17
Rice, Tamir, 6, 12
Richardson, Gloria, 28
riots, after death of King, M. L. Jr., 88. *See also* Baltimore riots
RNC. *See* Republican National Committee
Robinson, Pearl (aunt of Ryan, A.), 113
Rodham, Dorothy (mother of Clinton, H. R.), 73–75
Romans, book of, 75
Romney, Mitt, 19
Roosevelt, Eleanor, 103–4
Rowell, Dorothy, 116
Rowell, Victoria, 116, 121–22
Ryan (older daughter), 10, 32–33, 79, *p7*, *p8*; Baltimore riots and, 35–36; doll chosen by, 102; with Obamas, *p5*, *p6*
Ryan, April, 5, 9–10, *p1–p2*, *p4–p8*; mother of, 28, 78–80, 109–10; pregnancy, 79
Ryan, Robert, Jr., *p3*

Ryan, Robert, Sr., (father of Ryan, A.), *p2*, *p3*

Saltonstall, David, 51
Sanders, Bernie, 71
Sandtown Winchester, 87
Sankofa Experience, 119
Schmoke, Kurt, 10, 87
schools, 43; integration in, 98
Seale, Bobby, 115
segregation, 76, 98, 114–15
self-esteem, 99–101
Selma, 89; housing projects in, 44
sharecroppers, 8, 67
shootings, Walbrook Junction, 94–98. *See also* police shootings
Silent Protest Parade, 83
Simpson, O. J., 21, 60
single mothers, 7, 110, 118; statistics and, 23, 31
single-parent households, 7
Smitherman, Geneva, 47
SNCC. *See* Student Nonviolent Coordinating Committee
Spelling, Aaron, 62
statistics: being seen as, 29, 31–33; Black women's earnings, 22–23; Hispanic women's earning, 23; invisibility and Black women, 21; Jarrett on, 30–31; marriage and divorce, 28; minority children, 66; minority preschooler expulsion, 43; mothers and, 23, 31; population percentage of Black women, 24–25; US population, 21, 24–25; word, 30
Steele, Michael, 51
Student Nonviolent Coordinating Committee (SNCC), 27–28, 68
stuffed animals, 101
success, 111
Sykes, Wanda, 51–52

"the talk," 5–9, 102; Baltimore riots creating need for, 10, 11, 12; Lewis, J. R., on, 69

Taylor, Robert Robinson, 29–30
Taylor Bowman, Barbara, 30
"10 Reasons You'll Love Living in a
    Majority-Minority America" (Planas/
    Moreno), 66–67
Tio Pepe (restaurant), 13–14
Towns, Ed, 18
truck driver, with Confederate flag,
    11–12, 36
Truman, Harry, 81–82
Trump, Donald, 19, 62, 124–25
Truth, Sojourner, 119
Tubman, Harriet, 27, 50

uncle, shooting incident involving,
    94–98
Underground Railroad, 27
United States (US): majority-minority
    status, 66–67; population, 21, 24–25

value, 117, 119
Vanzant, Iyanla, 31, 36, 40, 110–11,
    123; on culture, 112; "great mother"
    and, 120; on n-word, 60; professional
    white attire of, 104–5
videos, 38, 40
Voting Rights Act, 9, 57, 70, 83

Walbrook Junction, 94–98
Walker, C. J., 27, 82–83
Wallace, George, 76
Washington, Booker T., 30
Washington Carver, George, 2

Washington Post, 5, 42, 49–50
water fountains, 114–15
WHCA. *See* White House
    Correspondents' Association
White House correspondent, 3, 28–29,
    79
White House Correspondents'
    Association (WHCA) dinner, 49–55
White House Council for Women and
    Girls, 29, 31
Williams, Armstrong, 51
Williams, Cindy, 77
Williams, Frances, 77
Willstein, Matt, 50
Wilmore, Larry, 49–55
Wilson, Woodrow, 83
Wolfers, Justin, 7, 24
women: earning statistics for Hispanic,
    23; history and, 17. *See also* Black
    women; mothers
"Women of Color and the Gender
    Wage Gap," 22–23
work-life balance, 109–16; community
    support in, 112–13; personal
    experience of, 109–10; Ryan, V.,
    example of, 109–10
World War I, 83
World War II, 72, 74

Yoruba priestess, 104–5
youth, fight for equality and, 120

Zimmerman, George, 39

About the Author

April Ryan, a 30-year journalism veteran, has been the White House correspondent for 20 years for American Urban Radio Networks (AURN), covering three US presidents who have called on her by name. She is also the Washington Bureau Chief. Along with responsibilities at the White House, Ryan hosts the daily feature, "The White House Report," which is broadcast to AURN's nearly 300 affiliated stations nationwide. She is regularly featured on political news shows and is a frequent speaker around the country. Her first book, *The Presidency in Black and White,* was published in 2015. She lives in Baltimore, Maryland, and is the proud mother of two girls.

—